RAILROAD

SHUTTERBUG

Jim Fredrickson stands beside a new F-3 type road diesel in the 1940s.

RAILROAD
SHUTTERBUG

Jim Fredrickson's Northern Pacific

Jim Fredrickson

WSU
PRESS

Washington State University Press
Pullman, Washington

Washington State University

Washington State University Press
PO Box 645910
Pullman, WA 99164-5910
Phone: 800-354-7360
Fax: 509-335-8568
E-mail: wsupress@wsu.edu
Web site: www.wsu.edu/wsupress

Library of Congress Cataloging-in-Publication Data

Fredrickson, Jim.
    Railroad shutterbug : Jim Fredrickson's Northern Pacific / by Jim Fredrickson.
      p. cm.
    ISBN 0-87422-195-1 (alk. paper) — ISBN 0-87422-197-8 (pbk. : alk. paper)
    1. Northern Pacific Railroad Company—History. I. Title.

HE2791.N855 F74 2000
385'.09795—dc21

00-043518

Front cover: NP 2261 and crew of train Number 4 at Stampede, June 2, 1944.
Back cover: NP's *North Coast Limited* at King Street Station, Seattle, December 19, 1969.

RESTRICTED SUBJECTS

Amateur photographers have many liberties in this country because it is a free country. To keep it free, don't help our enemies by violating any of these restrictions.

Restricted Areas—Coastal and other wide areas from which cameras are banned by special order.

Posted Areas—Where signs forbid taking pictures or carrying cameras, as at Navy yards, air fields, arsenals, munitions plants, Military or Naval experimental stations, etc.

Troops—Movements of Military or Naval organizations, troop trains, troops entraining or embarking or detraining or debarking. No objection to individuals or small numbers of soldiers at home, or at, or near home station, or on domestic police duty.

Airplanes—Pictures of airplanes at military flying fields or of the fields themselves or air views of any flying field, civil or military. Army transport planes at civil as well as military fields.

Aerial Views and Those Taken from Heights—Taking pictures from airplanes or taking cameras up into the air is prohibited except with special permission. Views from high places which may reveal information of value to the enemy also are forbidden.

Ships—Pictures of U. S. Naval or Merchant vessels at sea, in port, or at dock, and of ships of any nations opposing the Axis powers; mine fields; Army bases and ports of embarkation.

Industrial Plants—Interior views or air views of war production plants.

Fortifications—Anti-aircraft guns in place, bomb shelters or camouflaged objects with details which reveal their location, tank traps, beach wire, or any obstacles to an invading force.

Processing—Send films of military subjects that can be photographed only to reliable processing concerns. Harmless prints, furnished to Axis agents by subsidized companies, may be pieced together to reveal valuable information.

Copyright 1942 by *POPULAR PHOTOGRAPHY*, Ziff-Davis Publishing Company

WARTIME REGULATIONS FOR THE PHOTOGRAPHER

A digest of Federal Laws and Regulations covering pictures amateur photographers can and cannot take in wartime.

★

"Subjects not prohibited within the meaning of the Code of War Time Practices may be photographed."
THE WAR DEPARTMENT
Bureau of Public Relations

★

"The Government has no intention of discouraging picture-taking . . ."
THE OFFICE OF CENSORSHIP

Compiled by the editors of
POPULAR PHOTOGRAPHY

UNRESTRICTED SUBJECTS

There is no ban on carrying and using cameras in public places by persons other than enemy aliens. It is not forbidden to photograph views or objects except Military or Naval establishments or activities or equipment therein, or war production activities, or other restricted subjects which might convey information of value to the enemy.

Any of the following subjects can be photographed without violating the law, as long as they are not located in restricted areas.

Action subjects
Animals—farm, zoo, and home
Architectural subjects
Babies and children
Bathers
Beaches (except where restricted)
Birds
Cathedrals and churches
Circuses
Cliffs and rocks
Cloud formations
Cyclists
Desert scenes
Farm subjects
Family groups
Figure studies
Flowers
Games
Gardens
Groups
Homes
Horse-racing
Indoor subjects
Industrial scenes (except war work)
Lake scenes
Landscapes
Models
Mountain scenes
Nature studies
Oddities
Park scenes
Portraits, outdoor
Railroads (except where restricted)
Sailing craft

EASTMAN KODAK STORES, Inc. 910 Broadway Tacoma, Wash.

These are only a few of the many types of pictures that can be taken. Any subjects which are not specifically prohibited, and which do not convey information which might be of use to the enemy, are legitimate picture material.

●

Restricted Areas—It is up to the photographer to find out whether he is in a restricted area. Local authorities will provide this information.

●

Don't Conceal Cameras—Cameras should be carried openly at all times.

●

Carry Identification—Carry adequate means of identification when taking pictures.

●

When in Doubt—Remember that the purpose of all wartime regulations is to withhold information of value to the enemy. Don't take pictures that might reveal important information if they should fall into the hands of an enemy agent.

Rules for amateur photographers during World War II.

Acknowledgments

*O*ne day in May 1983, treasurer Les Greenwood and Education Committee chairman Duke Tone of BN West Credit Union in Tacoma were exploring ways of expanding their monthly newsletter, *The Chronicle*. They approached me with the idea of using photos I had taken during my railroad career. They were longtime friends (we had been NP telegraphers together) and I was most willing to supply pictures. The original intent was to write a short caption with each photo, but the flood of memories they brought back soon resulted in full-blown essays.

As the series grew, Dan Fiorino, Jan Smillie, and Denise Whitney of BN West suggested that the photos and stories might be the basis for a book. I am most grateful to Dave Nicandri, director of the Washington State Historical Society, for suggesting the WSU Press. Editor Glen Lindeman and designer Dave Hoyt are railfans at heart and a real pleasure to work with. Support from Pullman businessman Ken Vogel, grandson of NP Engineer George Hogan, was most helpful in getting the project rolling.

I would like to express my appreciation to NP veterans Albert Farrow, Warren McGee, and the late Ronald Nixon for blazing the trail and to the Northern Pacific Railway Historical Association for keeping the torch burning. And finally, thanks to my wife Cereta for supporting my devotion to NP for so many years and to my wonderful family for being along for the ride—sons Jim and Tim, daughter Kim, daughter-in-law Eileen, and grandchildren Eric, Jamie, Julie, and Timothy.

The stories are presented for the most part as they appeared in *The Chronicle*. There have been countless changes in the railroad scene since they were written. And, unfortunately, a number of my NP friends I wrote about are no longer with us. They are profoundly missed.

—*Jim Fredrickson*

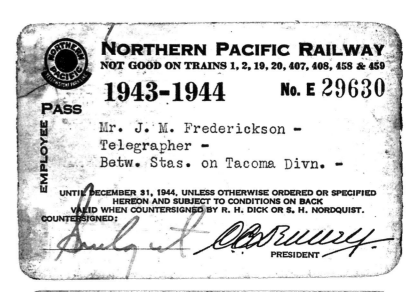

I started my career as a telegrapher in 1943.

I was born in Tacoma, Washington, on December 19, 1926, and lived my childhood years through the depths of the Great Depression. My father was a longshoreman and a prolonged strike in the early 1930s made these tough times even more desperate for my family. There was scarcely enough money for the bare necessities, so I started earning my own spending money at a very early age. My first venture was picking blackberries in vacant lots and selling them door-to-door, but this was limited to the summer season. I needed something to sell during the fall and winter.

Peddling magazines was the answer and I once again started door-to-door selling of the *Saturday Evening Post, Ladies Home Journal, Liberty,* and *Country Gentlemen*. This was no get-rich-quick scheme as the profit was barely a penny per five-cent magazine. Finding people who could afford to pay even this small amount during those times took lots of walking and doorbell ringing. However, there was a small extra incentive to keep trying—with bonus coupons from making sales, I could select from a catalog of prizes. With my coupons I chose a small plastic camera (market value nineteen cents) and a picture developing kit as my reward. It is incredible to realize that such a casual decision at such an early age could have had such a lasting, lifelong effect.

I graduated from selling magazines to being a *Tacoma News Tribune* paperboy. With the higher pay, I bought a better camera and, to make a long story short, became hooked on photographing steam locomotives, probably as a result of passenger train trips to the Midwest to visit my grandmother. This phase of my hobby found me spending lots of time trackside at the Tacoma Union Station.

Finally, one of the crew of a passenger train, Conductor Ed Jensen or Engineer George Voerge, said the fateful words, "You're always hanging around here, kid, you might as well go to work."

They took me upstairs and introduced me to Chief Dispatcher Austin Ackley, who no doubt was reluctant to hire a green sixteen year old. But the year was 1943 and with so many men away at war, the labor shortage was critical. He put me to work as a call boy. Call boys telephoned conductors, brakemen, engineers, and firemen to notify them an hour-and-a-half in advance of the time they were scheduled for duty on a train. In pre-telephone days, call boys did their notifying on foot.

From that start, I went to being a telegraph operator, then train dispatcher, night chief dispatcher, and finally Transportation Assistant in Seattle after the Burlington Northern merger in early 1970. I spent thirty-nine years on the railroad—all because of earning a camera selling magazines.

I once was told that while I was standing by the track with my camera, waiting to photograph an oncoming train, the fireman would say to the engineer, "There's that kid with the camera!"

It has all happened so quickly.

Class A-2 locomotive on the North Coast Limited *at Butte, Montana, in 1936—I took my first locomotive photo when traveling to Nebraska to visit my grandmother.*

NP 2600 at South Tacoma, Washington, June 29, 1946.

The Northern Pacific shops at South Tacoma were a major Tacoma industry for almost one hundred years. As many as 1,200 workers were on the payroll, building and repairing freight and passenger cars, and overhauling all of the locomotives on the west end of the railroad.

I toured the shops in 1939 with one of my classes at Jason Lee Junior High School, and the giant hammers and white-hot steel beams made a lasting impression. I later bowled in a Northern Pacific sponsored league with spirited competition between teams from the shops and the teams from downtown.

This 1946 photo shows Class A passenger locomotive 2600 receiving finishing touches outside Machine Shop Number 2 after a complete overhaul. The 2600 was the first 4-8-4 locomotive ever built. This design was later adopted by most of the major railroads and given the name "Northern" type because of its origin on the Northern Pacific. It was built by Alco-Schenectady (no. 67010) in 1926 and dismantled at South Tacoma, February 7, 1956.

NP Mobase Local leaving Tacoma, February 24, 1953.

The Northern Pacific started construction in Washington in 1871 at Kalama and reached Tacoma in 1873. An 1882 NP timetable did not bother to include train schedules for this far-away part of the railroad system, but its map shows the line going through the towns of Carrols, Monticello, Cowlitz, Castle Rock, Olequa, Grand Prairie, Winlock, Newaukum, Skookumchuck, Tenino, Yelm Prairie, and Lake View. The first segment north from Tacoma was completed to Wilkeson in 1877 and the track from Meeker to Seattle was not finished until 1883.

During the early construction period, a drawbridge was built across the city waterway in Tacoma. In 1893 it was replaced by the bridge in this photo. This was a heavily used bridge even after the construction of the Point Defiance Line in 1914 took away most of the NP and all of the Union Pacific traffic. Great Northern trains to Portland used the old original Prairie Line from 1910 until 1943; NP troop trains to Fort Lewis, Hoquiam-bound passenger trains, and Tacoma to East Auburn passenger train connections ran via the Drawbridge Line until the mid-50s. This 1953 photo of the Mobase Local was taken from the 15th Street UP drawbridge (since removed). From then until shortly after the Burlington Northern merger, the only regular train over the drawbridge was the Mobase Local, named after the Motor Base (later Mount Rainier Ordnance Depot) at Fort Lewis.

In 1971 the drawbridge was dismantled to remove overhead clearance restrictions on the Point Defiance main line. Afterward, the Mobase Local lingered on, giving freight service to Fort Lewis and the Prairie Line stations. In 1983, its crew consisted of Engineer F.H. Trentman, Fireman C.R. Rayment, Conductor R.D. Marshall, and brakemen D.G. Hayner and J.C. Wagner.

Agent Frank Emerick at NP's Nisqually Station, Washington, January 21, 1944.

When I started railroading in 1943 almost every town had its depot and agent, and also often had around-the-clock telegraph operators to deliver train orders and report passing trains. In fact, before automatic block signal systems became common in the early 1920s, there was a station about every six miles on the main line.

The beginning of the end of most of these stations was the coming of the diesel locomotive with longer and fewer trains. Centralized traffic control, train radios, microwave, computers, and centralized accounting all dealt death blows to the small station.

South Tacoma, McCarver Street, Sixth Avenue (Titlow), Steilacoom, Lakeview, Fort Lewis, Puyallup, Sumner, and Orting are among the Tacoma-area communities that had their own depots. This photo, with Agent Frank Emerick standing by the train order signal, was taken in January 1944, when I was working second trick at Nisqually. Mr.

Emerick began telegraphing for the Northern Pacific in 1914 after trying show business as a circus comedian and vaudeville dancer. Will Rogers and Al Jolson were among his friends during his pre-railroad career. He studied law and passed the bar exam but preferred to stay with the railroad. His legal experience served him well during his many years as Local Chairman for the Order of Railroad Telegraphers.

He did not seem at all handicapped by the loss of his right arm in a train accident. I remember being fascinated by his dexterity in tying a loop in a train order string. A truly remarkable and multi-faceted personality. After he passed away, his wife Martha continued to reside in Lakewood.

The small stations and the people who worked in them are a symbol of what life was like before America became automated. I feel fortunate to have been a part of it.

NP 5112 on curve at Wymer Station between Yakima and Ellensburg, Washington, June 5, 1944.

My first assignment after graduating from Stadium High School in June 1945 was second trick at Wymer, a telegraph station in the Yakima River canyon halfway between Ellensburg and Yakima. This area had a reputation for its numerous rattlesnakes and the regular operators amused themselves by terrifying newcomers with snake stories:

"You aren't going to use that sleeping bag, are you, kid? Rattlesnakes love to crawl into them when the sun goes down!"

"Be careful when you open a desk drawer. There might be a snake in it."

"Watch out when you climb up on the train order platform. Snakes like to sun themselves there."

I was nervous every minute I was at Wymer and didn't stray too far from the depot with my camera. Fortunately, I did take one of my all-time favorite photos (and close to the depot!)—a massive Class Z-6 locomotive leaning around the curve on an eastbound freight.

How many rattlesnakes did I see during my stay at Wymer? None!

In 1945 there were thirteen stations between Auburn and Yakima, but as train traffic diminished after World War II, they were closed one by one. Wymer shut down on December 25, 1957. In 1983, only Lester, Easton, and Ellensburg were left when the Burlington Northern virtually eliminated all trains from the old Northern Pacific First Subdivision. Then these three stations, too, were closed.

NP Centralia to South Bend mixed train at Frances, Washington.

This photo, taken on March 15, 1954, shows the South Bend mixed train stopping for passengers at Frances. On the same day, the following sad but true editorial, titled "Mister, That's the Last Train," appeared in the Portland *Oregonian:*

Come Saturday and the last passenger train will make its last run over the Northern Pacific's South Bend branch. It is tragic news, yet it will startle no one, for we have become too used to these disasters, fruits of the motor age.

It is evident that the pattern of railroad decay begins with the branches. Passenger service is reduced, then eliminated. Often the freight service follows the varnish trains. Then the branch is abandoned, the rails pulled up, while the kindly alder and fireweed attempt to hide the naked lie of a surviving sign that says to Look Out for Engine.

Though the South Bend branch will continue as a freight hauler, its life really ceased with the last passenger train; or so it will seem to us who rode the branch when the cars were four and even five. You could have your breakfast then at the depot dining room in Centralia and mount the South Bend Flyer on the sidetrack. The badge on the conductor's cap shone like silver, and the brakeman announced that this was the train for Chehalis, for Raymond, South Bend and all w-a-a-y points.

The way points were many, and mostly as busy as could be at making lumber: Littell, Dryad and Doty; Pe Ell, which turned out more crossarms than Western Union could use; then more mills at McCormick, Walville, Globe and Lebam. And do not forget the flagstops like Adna and Ceres, Frances, Nallpee and Menlo, where poor Willie Keil of the Aurora colonists lies beneath a cedar on a farmhouse hill. And blow once for unique Pluvius, whose founder said it was rained upon 362 days a year and the other three were as cloudy as night.

The metropolis of the branch was Raymond, where the sea gulls gathered at the depot when they saw Billy, who met all trains, coming with his hand-truck; and a moment later the Flyer's whistle let go at Willapa, telling all she was on time and rolling fast, while the town characters came to see the cars come in. It was a great moment, repeated continuously for nigh sixty years. All who rode that last train or see it pass now will be as dated as their grandparents, who wept to see the last stagecoach, just before the Iron Horse took over.

One hopes that the Flyer passes her last whistle-post with the steam dome rocking and the magic sound pealing out in volume to be heard by ships at sea, and by cougars on the mountain. And may the echoes reach that Valhalla where live the shades of the train crew who rode first over the South Bend Branch when the world was young, the skies were blue and steam was king.

NP freight train collision at Auburn, Washington, August 24, 1944.

My introduction to photographing train wrecks came at Auburn Yard on August 24, 1944. Any derailment is an awesome sight, but this collision was spectacular as it involved three trains. Switch engine 1268 was intending to go around the wye toward East Auburn, but a "boomer" switchman lined the wrong switch and sent it into the path of First 679 on the northbound main track. Engine 1777 on First 679 was rolled over into the side of Second 680 on the southbound track, derailing several cars on this train. Engineer Art McKay on the 1268 was seriously injured, but fortunately there were no fatalities. Chet Connick was the conductor of First 679 and Charlie Hoffman was the engineer. Second 680 had Conductor C.J. Hicks and Engineer Arvid Hansen aboard. Don Granger was foreman of the 1268's crew.

PTA convention special at Kanaskat, Washington, en route to Yakima, May 4, 1953.

It would be safe to say that the first twenty years of my photo collection covers the greatest period of change in railroad history. This picture of a PTA convention special train passing through Kanaskat can never be duplicated. Shriners, Rotary, Kiwanis, Parent-Teachers Association, and other convention goers now use the Interstate Highway system or a Boeing jet. Before Air Force 1, the President of the United States traveled in a special train labeled POTUS (President of the United States) and troop trains inundated the rail lines during World War II.

Engine 2626 in this picture often was used for special trains and always for the more important ones such as POTUS. In the early 1980s, specials were not completely extinct—Senator Warren Magnuson chartered a train during his last campaign, and the Ringling Brothers Circus moved in its own train. Freight train specials were less of a rarity, notably the infamous White Trains, which carried Trident missile motors through our region to the Bangor submarine base. Railfan specials, of course, have thrived in recent years.

NP station at Eagle Gorge, Washington, December 19, 1943.

I will not wash my face, I will not brush my hair,
I pig around the place, there's nobody to care,
Nothing but rock and tree, nothing but hill and stone,
Oh God but it's hell to be alone, alone, alone.

This verse from "The Telegraph Operator" by Robert W. Service must have been inspired by a station similar to the one at Eagle Gorge. The telegraph office, waiting room, and living quarters for the operators were all crammed into this single building. (There was one other small structure across the tracks with a crescent cut above its door.) There was no electricity, and illumination was by kerosene lamp. Coal stoves and ranges fulfilled heating and cooking needs. The local passenger trains provided the only means of getting in and out of Eagle Gorge as the nearest highway was eight miles away at Kanaskat. This really didn't matter much as the seven-day work week didn't give the operators much time to go anyplace anyway.

There was one reward for living under these isolated conditions—it was a fisherman's paradise. The depot actually was built partially over the Green River, which closely paralleled the tracks from Kanaskat to Lester. Every morning during the fishing season, fishermen lined up at Kanaskat to buy tickets on Number 4 to Eagle Gorge, Baldi, Humphrey, Sweeney's Ranch, Maywood, Nagrom, Hot Springs, and Lester. After a day of fishing on the river, they returned on Number 5.

The undisputed King of the River was R.B. Lewis who learned every inch of the Green River during his days as a telegraph operator, and knew better than anyone where the most and biggest trout were lurking. This was also, in my opinion, the most scenic stretch of the entire Northern Pacific. There were eight bridges across the Green River between Kanaskat and Lester and two tunnels with bridges over the river on each end.

The fishing and the scenery have been only memories since 1959 when the Howard Hanson Dam flooded the old line. The track was raised to its present higher location with access tightly restricted by the City of Tacoma water department.

This photo has a special meaning to me—it was taken on December 19, 1943, my seventeenth birthday.

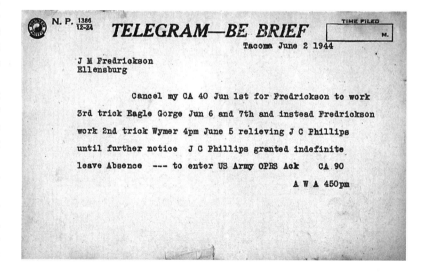

N. P. 1386
12-24

TELEGRAM—BE BRIEF

TIME FILED
M.

Tacoma June 2 1944

J M Fredrickson
Ellensburg

Cancel my CA 40 Jun 1st for Fredrickson to work 3rd trick Eagle Gorge Jun 6 and 7th and instead Fredrickson work 2nd trick Wymer 4pm June 5 relieving J C Phillips until further notice J C Phillips granted indefinite leave Absence --- to enter US Army OPRS Ack CA 90

A W A 450pm

NP 1783, Class W-3, at Tacoma Roundhouse, March 3, 1954.

Before the arrival of the first road diesels in 1944, the backbone of the Tacoma Division engine fleet was the "Mike"; short for Mikado, a name which came from its first appearance on the Nippon Railway in Japan in 1897. Although locomotive types had names, they were more technically described by their wheel arrangement—a Mikado being a 2-8-2, which meant there were a pair of leading wheels, eight drive wheels (four on each side) and two trailing wheels. Each railroad had its own method of classifying locomotives, usually with a letter and a number. For example, 2-8-2s were in the "W" series on the NP, "O" on the GN, and "L" on the Milwaukee. NP Class W-3 engine 1783 posed for this photo at the Tacoma Roundhouse in 1954.

NP locomotive historian Ronald Nixon said in his article for *Tell Tale* magazine: "No doubt the W-3 has done more for the Northern Pacific than any other class of locomotive. An inconspicuous workhorse, the W-3 hauled practically all of the through freight for a quarter of a century, and proved to be one of the most versatile steam locomotives ever used."

This was especially true west of the Cascades, where the modern giants like the Z-6s and A-4s were never used. W-3s not only pulled the hot-shot 679s and 680s between Seattle and Portland, but also were used on the heavier branch lines such as Sumas, Hoquiam, and Bangor. Their versatility also found them extensively used on troop trains (during World War II some railroads, UP for one, rechristened their Mikados as "MacArthurs"), and in helper service at Centralia and Woodinville. There were 135 W-3s on the NP roster along with 25 similar W-5s and 200 lighter Mikados in the W, W-1, and W-2 series. Six 2-8-2 switch engines in the W-4 series made for a total of 366 Mikados on the Northern Pacific, all built by the American Locomotive Company between 1904 and 1923. But, for some unknown reason, on this end of the railroad, the W-3s were the only ones affectionately called "Mike."

Appropriately, the last steam train on the Tacoma Division, a "Farewell to Steam Special" on December 8, 1957, was pulled by the NP 1776, a W-3.

NP Santa Claus train with doubleheader engines 2626 and 2601 at Lester, December 13, 1955.

The holiday season invariably brings back a flood of memories of some of the more agonizing hours during my twenty-four years as a train dispatcher. Dispatchers don't have to contend with the physical discomforts of wintertime railroading as do trainmen, switchmen, section men, and signal maintainers, but mental challenges can be unrelenting. A dispatcher's basic duty is to predict where two opposing trains will meet and at what time, and arrange for one of them to be on a siding when this occurs. In this present age of electronic miracles, dispatchers in main-line territory have a track layout display in front of them with lights indicating the locations of trains. By pushing a button, a dispatcher can set the switches for a train to take to a siding.

Back in my ancient time, the dispatcher dictated written "train orders" to telegraph operators at the few and far between stations in his territory and these orders told trains where to stop and enter a siding for a "meet." With no radio communication and the long distances between offices, decisions had to be made far in advance.

At best, this planning wasn't easy, and the variables caused by winter conditions made things even worse. Wet and icy rails made train running times more uneven, small snow slides disrupted the block signal system, and, when heavy snows came, work trains with spreaders and rotaries really messed up a railway. In the midst of all this came the Christmas mail. In those days, almost all mail moved by rail and the holiday volume was so heavy that NP put on an extra mail train each way two weeks before Christmas. These were known as the Santa Claus specials.

The eastbound Santa operated as a second section of the *Mainstreeter,* and the westbound normally ran just ahead of the westward *Mainstreeter* and the *North Coast Limited.* The meeting point of the Santa specials usually was in the long, dark canyon between Ellensburg and Yakima. Several other uncertainties helped make this nail-biting time for a dispatcher—how long would Santa East be at Ellensburg working the mail, and how long would Santa West be at Yakima? (The orders had to be ready before the trains arrived at these stations.) Throw in a freight train or two in the territory and the situation became really tense.

All in all, the extra challenge made the job more interesting and far from boring. When things worked out well, it made for a good feeling of accomplishment.

23

"North Coast Limited" connection approaching Tacoma, March 15, 1953.

In the late Nineteenth Century, the original main line of the Northern Pacific went through Enumclaw, Buckley, and Orting into Tacoma. Passengers for Seattle were obliged to take other secondary lines to reach their destination. With the building of the Palmer Cutoff in 1900, however, the NP main-line passenger trains began running directly into Seattle via Ravensdale and Auburn. Tacoma was not completely left out, as connecting service was provided from East Auburn by especially assigned two- and three-car trains.

Each crew assignment called for making at least two trips a day between Tacoma and Auburn. For example, one crew would run from Tacoma to East Auburn with passengers for the evening Spokane Local, bring back passengers from the westbound local from Spokane, then return several hours later with passengers for the *North Coast Limited*.

These jobs were done by the vaudeville crews—terminology borrowed from the Pennsylvania Railroad which had many similar short intermittent passenger runs. These were likened to the life of a vaudeville performer who would do his act on stage, then wait several hours before going on again. I made a number of inquiries among veteran railroaders searching for the origin of the vaudeville name, and finally Chuck Hough and Ralph Amundson provided the answer. They worked as extras on the vaudeville runs in their younger days, but the regular crews for these choice jobs were "old heads" like conductors Bennie Eckler, Harry Wedeen, Joe Anderson, C.P. Hough, and "Carnation" Bob Hutchison; brakemen Walter Knoell, Stephen Van Volkenburg, Ed Darland, Glen Helmer, and Lynn Smith; and engineers Bert Miller, Max King, and Adolph Zuegner.

One vaudeville crew had a great impact on my life. As I mentioned earlier, it was Conductor Ed Jensen and Engineer George Voerge on the evening connection who saw me hanging around the depot with my camera and finally decided I should go to work for the railroad. They introduced me to Chief Dispatcher Austin Ackley, and on April 18, 1943, my thirty-nine year career had its start at the caller's desk in the Union Station.

The East Auburn connections finally became victims of our sometimes reverse progress and were replaced by buses on August 25, 1954.

NP 2261 and crew of train Number 4 at Stampede, June 2, 1944.

This photo, technically and artistically speaking, may not be one of my "best," but for fond, personal memories it's hard to beat. During my early days as an extra board operator I didn't own an automobile, which was no great problem as local passenger train service provided adequate transportation. On this spring day in 1944, I was en route to Wymer on 4 when we were held at Stampede several hours because of a minor freight train derailment in the big tunnel. This delay gave me the opportunity to photograph not only the locomotive, but also the very notable crew members.

On the left is Conductor Bob Cameron, and on the right Brakeman Stephen Van Volkenburgh. (Flagman Bill Waldusky was back protecting the rear of the train and not available to pose for the photo.) These three worked together for many years and considered themselves "A to Z" men—everything neat and tidy and strictly according to the book. Mrs. Van Volkenburgh recalls her husband spending hours at a time polishing his shoes. Because of their immaculate appearance and many years of seniority, this crew was often held off their regular run to handle important special trains, such as President Franklin D. Roosevelt's super-secret rail visit to the Northwest in 1942 to inspect defense plants. Bob was "Number One" on the seniority list at the time of this picture, having started work on October 8, 1896—only eight years after the Stampede Tunnel was finished. Van worked for a year as a street car conductor in Tacoma, then went braking for the NP on September 27, 1909. I remember him telling about being selected to stand at the steps of the *North Coast Limited* when it was on display at the Tacoma Union Station during opening week in 1911.

The engine crew on this day was Fireman Ed Doran on the left and Engineer Ed Foisie on the right. Because of my interest in photographing locomotives, I became well acquainted with all of the engineers on the division and found myself riding in the engines more than in the coaches, especially if Ed Foisie was in charge. I have enough memories of riding with Ed to almost fill a book—such as stopping at an Eagle Gorge logging camp so the fireman, Ed Doran, could run over to the cookhouse and get an apple pie for us. The NP was blessed with many fine engineers while I was Mountain Dispatcher, but I never saw one quite the equal of Ed when it came to making up time with a late train. He was spectacular. He told me once that a road foreman had scolded him for running too fast, and his response was "little Jimmy expects me to run that fast and that's how fast I'm going to run."

He constantly chewed Black Jack gum (whatever became of it?) and one time after an especially fine run I had the operator at Auburn include a pack with his train orders. Ed took an early interest in the labor movement and for many years was local chairman of the Brotherhood of Locomotive Firemen and Enginemen. His son, Chuck, recalls his father being noted for his popularity and fairness, both with the company and the men. In his early years, Ed attended a steam engineering school conducted by the YMCA in Boston, then went to work on the Panama Canal construction project for a year, before coming to Seattle where he hired on with the NP as an engine wiper, and then fireman on June 26, 1904.

The 2261 was one of forty Class Q-6 and similar Q-5 locomotives that were the NP's biggest and fastest passenger engines from 1920 until the coming of the "A" engines in 1926. 2261 was especially equipped for mountain tunnel service with a smoke deflector to protect the tunnel ceilings from the upward blast of smoke; glass covered the cab number so that soot and grime could be easily washed off. At the time this photo was taken, the headlight has a shroud to comply with World War II blackout regulations. Leaning against the "cowcatcher" is a hoop with a bag full of respirators— wet sponges in rubber face masks. The operators at Stampede and Martin handed them up to train crews entering the tunnel for breathing protection, in case the train stalled in the tunnel. The operators were paid a whopping $17.50 a month to wash the respirators and keep them sanitary. This wasn't an easy job as the respirators were made of white rubber and it took a lot of scrubbing with Sapolio to remove black fingerprints. The memories are endless . . .

President Harry S Truman's campaign train at Auburn, June 11, 1948.

The opponents in the 1948 presidential election were a complete contrast in style. Republican challenger Thomas E. Dewey was endowed with a rich baritone voice and his vocabulary and diction were considered to be "the most perfect type of American English." The opposite was true of President Harry S Truman. The moment he started to read a speech, his voice went flat and his delivery was monotonous. With his thick glasses, he had trouble returning to a line of text once he had raised his eyes to look at the audience. Bright lights also bothered him.

However, in earlier campaigns Truman had spoken effectively without relying on written speeches. His staff, too, observed that when talking extemporaneously to small groups in the White House, his wit, colloquialisms, and flourishes were captivating. Although by 1948 the airplane had become a principal means of travel, Truman preferred campaigning by train. "Whistle stop" speeches were his most effective means of communicating; large numbers of people, in those pre-television days, came to the stations to observe their president.

On the rear end of the train was Truman's car, the Ferdinand Magellan, which had been especially built for President Franklin Roosevelt at the cost to the government of one dollar. It was a model of comfort and safety. The underside had a shield to protect passengers from bomb blasts and the green-tinted windows were bulletproof. Viewed from the outside, the car's most striking feature was a canopied rear platform adorned with the presidential seal. Attached to the back railing was a lectern with a microphone connected to overhead loudspeakers.

Truman was invited to deliver the commencement address and receive an honorary degree at the University of California in June 1948. This provided an ideal opportunity for him to stump the country by rail. The Pacific Northwest was included in the itinerary. His speeches in Washington followed the pattern of those at other cross-country stops—he lambasted what he called "the do-nothing" Republican-controlled 80th Congress. Supposedly in Bremerton, someone in the audience first shouted "give 'em Hell, Harry!" and from then on those words symbolized his campaign. He spoke to a huge throng at 9th and Broadway when in Tacoma on June 11.

In southwest Washington, Mother Nature forced a change in plans for the POTUS special. The infamous 1948 Columbia River flood that wiped out Vanport between Vancouver and Portland also inundated the NP tracks in the Kalama area. Truman had to proceed to Portland by auto, while his train was pulled backwards from Tacoma to Auburn, where this photo was taken, and detoured to Portland via Pasco. As was usual for important specials, the 2626 was the assigned road engine, but with seventeen cars to pull, helper engine 1674 also was needed. The long passing-by of this train gave me ample time to rewind the film and photograph the president's car as it came by. Jet planes, of course, now take candidates to more places in much shorter time, but, as President Truman once said, it was "intriguing and helpful . . . for the President to get away from the White House and get to see the people as they are." How many people can be seen from Air Force One?

Great Northern train Number 671 derailed at Kyro, Washington, May 19, 1957.

This photo of a Great Northern derailment illustrates the dangers facing those who have chosen train and engine service as their career. Journals fail, wheels and rails break, and reckless automobile drivers try to beat trains at crossings. One wonders how anyone with any railroad knowledge could use the word "featherbedding" to describe these occupations.

In my ongoing search for railroad memorabilia, I ran across a 1906 letter written by the brother of a fireman on the Philipsburg, Montana, branch of the NP to his father in Iowa. It is a first-hand account of how risky the life of a fireman could be, but at the same time the letter is full of unintentional humor. Here it is, just the way it was written:

Philipsburg, Mont.
Dec. 6th, 1906

Dear Father,

I road down to Drummond and back with Sherman the 5th of this month and his Enginear told me that Sherman was as good a fireman that there was on the road and he is a dandy. You would not know him if you saw him. He don't look anything like he did when he was in the barber shop. He is big, stout and healthey. When I was agoing down with him the other day they went through a little town and they don't stop onless that someone wants to get on and they did not stop. But they haft to get their orders and a fireman hafto reach out for them. Well. Sherman was a throughing in coal and when he reached out for the orders he was too late and the train was agoing fast and he jump off of the engine and got the orders and caught the rear end and come awalking over the train to the engine. The train was agoing so fast if I had of got off I would probly broke my neck. Everybody likes Sherman in this country. His eyes is just as big as ever. I don't think there is much danger of Sherman getting hurt on the rail road. He throughes his coal and then gets his head a looking out of the cab. He is always a looking out of the cab. He is always a looking out for himself. When he was in that wreck he saw the other train was running fast and he jumped off and run up the side of a mountain and it was so steep that he had to go on his hands and nees. And he said car wheels and everything else was a flying around him.

I will write more soon. Don't show this to ma.
Your son,
Artista E. Sines

31

NP Number 5 at Wymer, May 19, 1944.

Selah, Wymer, Thrall, Ellensburg, Thorp, Cle Elum, Easton, Martin, Stampede, Lester, Hot Springs, Nagrom, Maywood, Sweeney's Ranch, Humphrey, Baldi, Eagle Gorge, Kanaskat, and Ravensdale—places where Northern Pacific's Number 5 obligingly stopped for people, mail, groceries, and anything else needed from the outside world. Fishermen in the summer, hunters in the fall, and skiers in the winter were regular patrons of this classic example of railroad passenger service when steam was "King."

Number 5 and its eastbound counterpart, Number 6, have special memories for me and any other telegrapher who depended on them to go to and from the remote assignments on the "Mountain." The pace was slow, the food in the cafe car outstanding, and the crews were (for the most part) warm and friendly. Bob Cameron, Horace Mann, Phil Moran, Charlie Sefton, and Lyle Wren were classic, fifty-year veterans of the rugged days of railroading. They looked so magnificent in their uni-forms with gold buttons and key chains, and service stripes and stars covering their sleeves. Ed Jensen had missing fingers from the days of link and pin couplers. And even "Roaring Bill" Ainsworth could be friendly in his own way.

The engineers were noted for their speed and skill. Bill Dahlberg was undoubtedly the best and routinely taken from his regular assignment to handle presidential and directors' specials. Louie Butt and Jack Hodder were two other "throttle artists" who made up time without slopping coffee in the diner. I was always amazed at Red Bevan roaring by the depot at Easton in a cloud of smoke, steam, dust, and cinders and still making a perfect stop at the water plug. Riding in the cab with my good friend Ed Foisie is at the top of my list of treasured memories, especially trips on Number 5.

Good ride, good food, good friends—what more could a kid who liked trains ask for.

Santa Claus at East Auburn, December 24, 1954, accompanied by an illustrious crew of helpers and entertainers.

On December 17, 1954, the following letter was sent to all of the elementary schools in the Auburn area:

Dear Teacher:

The boys and girls of your room and their little brothers and sisters are invited to the Northern Pacific Railway's East Auburn Station on Friday, December 24th, to see Santa Claus come in on the Vista Dome *North Coast Limited* at 2:00 p.m.

He told us that he plans to sing some Christmas Carols and play his violin too!! We got an advance look in that great big bag of his and we're positive there were lots of candy canes in there for distribution to all the boys and girls.

Plan to attend and be with Santa.

Very truly yours,
R.C. Bergum, Agent, NP Ry.

On December 24, Santa boarded Number 26 at Seattle and after visiting with the children on the train got off at East Auburn where he greeted four hundred boys and girls who responded to the invitation. The other eleven months of the year Santa went by the name Waino Hannus and was an NP clerk at Auburn. In 1918 when in his early teens, he had started working for the railroad weighing coal at Carbonado Station. He spent most of his career as a clerk at Enumclaw until the closing of that job forced a move to Auburn.

A fraternal lodge that Hannus belonged to needed a Santa Claus one Christmas and he volunteered, thoroughly enjoying the experience. His wife, Snelma, bought red velvet to make his first costume. He filled the role of Santa each December for many years, first for friends, relatives, and neighbors, and then schools, hospitals, nursing homes, and anywhere a truly dedicated, genuine-looking Santa was needed. He brought happiness to thousands and at the same time much goodwill for the Northern Pacific.

The Auburn Roundhouse Drum and Bugle Corps.

(left to right) Conductor Bennie Eckler, Special Agent Phil Morgan, Superintendent Worthington Smith, Trainmaster Dick Judson, and Auburn Roundhouse Foreman Gus Nelson.

Seattle's University Station, ca. 1941.

The UW Huskies and the NP had a close relationship in the days before widespread commercial airline service. College teams traveled by train when competing in other parts of the country. Normally, teams occupied Pullman sleepers on regularly scheduled trains, but for "big" games, such as the Rose Bowl, special trains for the teams and fans would be operated. In my collection, there is a Southern Pacific menu for "University of Washington Football Trains en route ROSE BOWL GAME, Pasadena, California, WASHINGTON vs. PITTSBURGH, January 1, 1937."

A photo of Coach James Phelan and the team is included inside the cover. The players' uniforms, complete with leather helmets, look ancient now. Breakfast prices in the menu range from 50 cents for fruit, muffins, and coffee, to 90 cents for ham, bacon or calf's liver, and eggs along with juice, cereal, and muffins.

The Huskies dominated the rowing world in the 1930s and the crews were dependent on the NP and other railroads to get them and their equipment to the regattas, notably the annual event held on the Hudson River at Poughkeepsie, New York. Crew coach Dick Erickson remembered the procedures for these complicated journeys. Shells were carried on the shoulders of the oarsmen up the hill from the crew house and spotted for loading on the UW campus power plant coal spur. During this era the NP tracks were still in place on the present Burke-Gilman Trail. The racing shells then were loaded into long, end-door passenger cars that had to be ordered for service long in advance because of their limited numbers. Shells built by George Pocock for other schools also would be loaded here. (On return trips, spruce was loaded in the baggage car in Montana to be used for making Pocock shells.) The usual thirty-six members of the Husky travelling group were seated in the diner one hour ahead of the regular passengers. Student managers would "bed down" in the baggage car with the shells.

The UW Associated Students had a unique idea for viewing crew races. They contracted NP to operate a special train made up with benches on flat cars to follow the shells at a point at Lake Washington close to the tracks. "Observation Train" tickets for the California-Washington Regatta, April 26, 1941, contain disclaimers for liability while boarding, riding, or leaving the train. This was a fine way to view races from start to finish, but the idea was short-lived; during a race on this exposed part of the lake a strong wind came up and sunk the shells. The Husky crew races since have been held on the sheltered Montlake Cut.

For many years, the public was served by the NP's University Stations adjacent to the campus. Railway Express was handled at the station and Christmas was Agent Fred Herberg's busiest time during the year. While attending the UW, I worked weekends for the NP and had my check sent to University Station.

NP Number 408 arriving at Tacoma, April 25, 1949.

Over the years, the Northwest region has had its share of fine names for trains—Northern Pacific's *North Coast Limited* and *Mainstreeter*, Great Northern's *Empire Builder* and *Western Star*, Union Pacific's *City of Portland* and *Portland Rose*, and Milwaukee's *Olympian* and *Columbian*.

However, one of the most spectacular passenger trains, shown here rounding a turn by a switchman's shanty at Tacoma in 1949, had only a number—it was 408 southbound, and 407 northbound. These trains were the NP's share of the Seattle-Portland pool passenger operation and they had the fastest schedule. They also were the connection for the Southern Pacific's *Cascade*, usually having four sleeping cars that went to and from California, plus two baggage cars, eight to

twelve coaches, and a parlor car. To provide food and beverages for the passengers, the train also included a Tavern Car, which was half luncheonette and half dining tables decorated in red leather upholstery—quite flamboyant for the usually conservative Northern Pacific. A train auditor as well as the regular conductor were needed on these runs to handle tickets for up to 1,200 passengers.

In addition to the 2626, Class "A" engines 2600, 2602, 2603, 2604, 2609, and 2610 were assigned at one time or another to these trains. As testimony to the efficiency of these locomotives, they handled fifteen to twenty cars on Number 408 from Seattle to Portland in four hours—exactly the same running time as the modern-day's shorter, diesel-powered *Coast Starlight*.

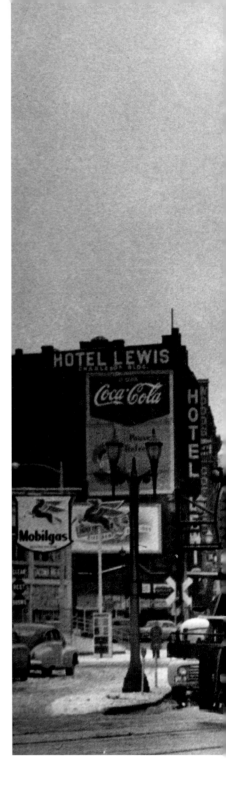

NP Number 422 leaving Tacoma, February 18, 1956.

This photo, taken on a dismal day, commemorates the end of branch-line passenger service in the State of Washington. Number 422 is shown crossing Tacoma's Pacific Avenue for the last time, on its way to Hoquiam with regular stops at South Tacoma, Lakeview, Fort Lewis, Nisqually, Saint Clair, Olympia, Gate, Elma, Montesano, and Aberdeen, and flag stops at Camp Murray, Union Mill, Lacey, Belmore, Little Rock, Mima, Oakville, Porter, Malone, Satsop, Brady, and Aberdeen Junction.

It is incredible now to look back at how many passenger trains were running before the automobile age sealed their doom. A Northern Pacific advertisement in the May 9, 1913, *Tacoma Daily News* proclaims "Four Trains Each Day to Portland; Three Daily to Aberdeen-Hoquiam. High-back seat coaches, Observation Cars, Dining Cars on Day Trains. Coaches and Standard, and Tourist Sleeping Cars on Night Trains. Electric Lights on All Trains." The employees' timetable for that year shows that, in addition to the four NP Portland trains, there were four OWR&N (UP) and three GN trains, for an unbelievable eleven trains each way—and this was before the opening of the Point Defiance Line—with all of them on the single track Prairie Line via Roy, Yelm, and Rainier. It must have been a train dispatcher's nightmare.

Two of the three Seattle to Hoquiam trains went through to Moclips. Hoquiam was also served by three OWR&N and two Milwaukee trains.

The Markham-Ocosta Branch had two passenger trains each way as did the South Bend Branch, the Elma-McCleary Branch, and the Fairfax Branch. Four trains each way ran from Centralia to Gate to connect with the Seattle to Hoquiam trains. Three trains each day ran from Tacoma to Kanaskat, Orting, Buckley, and Enumclaw, with one of them going through to Kerriston. All of these trains were met by connecting trains at Cascade Junction to take passengers to Burnett and Spiketon. The Yacolt Branch did not have full-fledged passenger trains, but two mixed trains each way from Vancouver carried passengers.

On the "north end" in 1913 there were two passenger trains each way on the NP from Seattle to Bellingham, and one a day each way from Seattle to Sumas, Darrington to Arlington, and North Bend to Seattle via Woodinville, Kirkland, and Renton. Mixed train service was provided on the Monte Cristo Branch. Most of the action was on the mountain main line, with six passenger trains each way between Auburn and Yakima.

The Great Northern was running four passenger trains each way daily between Seattle and Vancouver, BC, and two between Anacortes, Burlington, Concrete, and Rockport. The Bellingham Bay and British Columbia Railroad timetable shows three trains between Bellingham and Sumas with one of them going through to Glacier. The Columbia and Puget Sound ran two passenger trains from Seattle to Black Diamond and Franklin, as did the Tacoma Eastern from Tacoma to Mineral and Morton. And last and maybe least was the Port Townsend Southern with passenger trains between Tenino and Olympia and Port Townsend and Quilcene. And, all of this does not take into account the many interurban street car lines.

Sadly, this complicated narrative can be brought to a quick conclusion by quoting an Agatha Christie book title, *And Then There were None*.

Northern Pacific bowling league's Machine Shop team.

Shortly after World War II, Northern Pacific began sponsoring a ten-team bowling league for employees in the Tacoma area. This photo is the Machine Shop team from the South Tacoma Shops, one of the perennial powerhouses of the league. Left to right: John Ammann, Jim Kelly, Gordy Parker, Joe Desmond, and Bob Hall. The league first bowled at the South Tacoma Lanes at 52nd and South Tacoma Way, an old-time establishment with pin boys and a foul judge. (I remember the foul judge well, as he rang the gong on me five times in one game, resulting in a humiliating score of 56.)

After a few years, this building was turned into a Safeway store and the league moved to the old USO lanes at 9th and Pacific; then to the Broadway Bowl; and with the influx of new houses, found a final home at the Paradise Bowl until the league disbanded early in the 1960s.

A friendly but intense rivalry prevailed between the teams from South Tacoma—Machine Shop, Paint Shop, Pipefitters, Mill, and Blacksmith Shop, versus those from the downtown area—Accountants, Dispatchers, Rip Track, Yard Office, and Roundhouse. Work force reductions and realignments caused periodic changes with the Electricians, Baggagemen, Tacoma Freight House, Auburn Diesel Shop, and Store Department entering teams at various times during the league's history.

Of the bowlers in this photo, Bob Hall started as a laborer at South Tacoma in 1940, became an apprentice machinist, and, after time-out for the Navy during the war, became Diesel Shop Foreman at South Tacoma in 1960. In 1969 he was Mechanical Refrigerator Repair Foreman for the NP at Auburn and retired from the Burlington Northern as Foreman of Cars.

Gordon Parker went to work at South Tacoma in 1929 (!) as helper, then apprentice, and became a machinist in 1935 working for many years in the air brake department. After thirty-nine years at South Tacoma, he worked his final four years at Auburn with Bob in the mechanical refrigeration department. John Ammann, Jim Kelly, and Joe Desmond were all veteran machinists.

Those were the days, my friends . . . we thought they'd never end.

NP Class 3-6 5120 on westbound freight between Livingston and Bozeman, Montana, May 1954.

New Year Greetings

Away thru the night, with a rush and roar,
And the ruddy glare from the fire-box door;
Following the path of the headlight, clear,
Goes my wish to you for a Happy New Year.
—From an antique postcard, date and author unknown.

If there were a railroad photographers' hall of fame, the first inductees would include two NP veterans from Montana—Conductor Warren McGee of Livingston and Wire Chief Ron Nixon of Missoula-Polson.

Their artistic talent and dedication to historic preservation has provided a priceless legacy for future generations. For many years their incomparable photos were used by others in countless books and magazines. Finally, these two long-time friends produced a book of their own—*The Northern Pacific of McGee and Nixon*. It is a truly outstanding publication and a "must" for any railfan, or, for that matter, for anyone who appreciates outstanding photographic skill.

Another NP veteran nationally recognized for his many years of railroad photography has been the Northwest's own Albert Farrow, a retired engineer from Auburn. His specialty was logging roads and short lines, and a great majority of books on these subjects include his photos.

NP 1369 at 15th Street Tower, Tacoma, April 26, 1945.

This picture of a Class S-4 locomotive was taken on the day it was released from a complete overhaul at the South Tacoma Shops. Steam locomotive boilers were filled with small tubes called "flues" that connected the firebox at the rear of the engine with the smoke box at the front. The flues were completely surrounded with water. Hot smoke and gasses from the fire passed through the flues en route to the smokestack and, in doing so, caused the water to boil creating steam for power. Federal regulations required that flues be removed every four years and thoroughly reconditioned or replaced. At the same time, all other parts of the engine were refurbished. The Northern Pacific had three major shops do this work—at South Tacoma for the west end, Livingston, Montana, for the central district, and Brainerd, Minnesota, for the east end.

The South Tacoma Shops were built in 1890 on 131 acres of ground—700 feet wide and 6400 feet long—extending from the Union Avenue viaduct to South 56th Street, and employing up to 1,300 workers. Locomotive repair was not its only function—a lumber mill produced 1.5 million board feet per month, and the New Car Shed could turn out ten boxcars, six refrigerator cars, and nineteen flat cars per day.

A 1940 "Progress" edition of the *Tacoma Times* gives a vivid description of this major industry:

> This veritable city of huge structures—13 brick and 11 wooden, house some 50 major fabricating and manufacturing industries. Cold statistics begin to pall as the visitor hears each new fact seemingly exceed human imagination. He'll see lumber stacked as high as in any sawmill; he'll see steel ingots, rods and plates being made into bolts, boilers, pumps, girders, railroad spikes; he'll see a huge and complicated machine shop—just for keeping the shop's tools in good order; he'll see a ponderous row of locomotives "with their clothes off and their innards scattered"; he'll see craftsmen carving wooden patterns; he'll see great "hammers" capable of a 2 1/2-ton wallop—cracking hazel nuts to show off. In short, the visitor who tours the wondrous shops of the Northern Pacific will discover a new world—a fascinating world of action, vital to Tacoma.

Little did that reporter know of the devastating effects that the diesel age would have.

The shiny paint on the 1369 shows that she has just emerged from her month-long shop ordeal. She has stopped at 15th Street during a day of running up and down the South Tacoma hill for "breaking in" to be sure everything is in good working order. Seated in the cab is engineer Archie Rhea, another page in my book of good memories. Firemen who worked with Archie say he was a real "throttle artist" who could get as much out of a steam engine as anyone on the Division. He had the knack of getting his engine "hooked up" just right and making it "purr like a sewing machine." He loved to run fast and took delight in making new firemen nervous, although his efficient throttle work made their job easy. He was a friend to all and famous for his generosity. NP veterans Charlie Moreau, Bill Boucher, Harry McLain, Bob Downey, Don Shane, and Jim Wyse shared their information with me about Rhea and the South Tacoma Shops.

NP 70, Class F-1 Baldwin "hog" at Chehalis, Washington, April 19, 1945.

Most of the NP's earlier locomotives were high-wheelers designed for service on the prairies where the minimal grades made speed more important than power. But when the rails reached the Rockies and Cascades, engines were needed that could "slug it out" on the tortuous grades over these foreboding barriers. To tackle this challenge, nine Consolidation type (2-8-0) locomotives with forty-nine inch drive wheels were ordered from the Baldwin Locomotive Works in 1883 designated as Class "F," followed by twenty-eight similar Class F-1 engines built from 1888 through 1891. Because of the comparatively small drive wheel diameter, they were slow moving, but extremely strong and sturdy, which soon earned them the nickname "hog."

NP historian Ron Nixon sent me a copy of a train order dated "Missoula, September 23, 1893," addressed to the agent at Arlee, Montana, which reads: "Call crew and 2 hogs for No. 56 at 9:00 PM." This unglamorous label stuck with them to the end of their existence in the late 1940s and does not give a true picture of the valuable service they performed for so many years.

The coming of the much bigger Mikado and Mallet engines shortly after the turn of the century put an end to the main-line chores for the hogs, but they spent many yeoman years thereafter on west-end branch lines with steep grades and heavy tonnage, such as the Darrington, Orting, and South Bend branches on the Tacoma Division, the Lewiston Branch on the Idaho Division, and the Wallace Branch on the Rocky Mountain Division. Engineer Charlie Everest, who started firing in 1918, spent many a sweaty hour both heaving coal into the firebox and pulling the throttle of hogs, and swore they could do "more work than any diesel." He backed up this claim by pointing out that hogs pulled one-hundred car log trains from Lake Kapowsin to Tacoma six days a week the year around.

It is a sad page in Northern Pacific history that so few examples of its fine steam locomotives were preserved as museum pieces. The NP 70, pictured here, was dismantled at South Tacoma on April 25, 1947. A hog with its ancient appearance and sixty-years service certainly should have been saved, instead of all going to the scrap heap. Engineer Al Farrow and his fellow members of the Northwest Railroad Historical Society almost succeeded in saving the 80—the NP loaned it to them in 1938, along with a day coach to use as a meeting place. The many hours they spent cleaning and polishing their hog were to no avail, as it was taken back to be part of the NP's contribution to the World War II scrap metal drive. Such a pity—if a movie version of the children's classic story, *The Little Engine That Could* is ever made, the 80 would have been an ideal candidate for the leading role.

UP 2203, NP 1670, and Milwaukee 1205 at Hoquiam, Washington, May 23, 1945.

At the end of 1944, I had finished high school and was ready to begin work full-time instead of just on weekends as I had done while in school. As an extra telegrapher, it didn't take me long to see a lot of the Tacoma Division, as I was sent to fourteen stations in the first five months of 1945—Nisqually, Lakeview, Stampede, Easton, Ellensburg, Millburn, Kelso, Martin, Thrall, Napavine, 15th Street Tower, Bucoda, Reservation, and Hoquiam.

So much activity occurred in such a short time that it makes it hard today to remember details except for two incidents. Upon entering the depot at Martin to work second trick on April 12, I was told that President Franklin D. Roosevelt had died. He was the only president within my memory and it was hard to imagine anyone else taking his place.

I also remember deadheading from Easton to Millburn via Trains 5, 414, and 402 to Chehalis and taking a taxi the remaining seven miles only to find that the Weyerhaeuser trains were not running and my services weren't needed.

On May 22, 1945, I began a one-week assignment on second trick at Hoquiam and while there took an unusual photo of locomotives from three different roads together at one time. The Union Pacific and Milwaukee trains used Northern Pacific tracks from Aberdeen to Hoquiam, and the engines of all three roads tied up at the NP roundhouse on adjacent tracks. NP Class W-1 engine 1670 would go out that evening on hotshot Number 696 taking the Grays Harbor, Elma branch, and Centralia business through to Auburn for connection that same night with Number 602, the premier transcontinental freight. Similar operations prevailed on the Union Pacific and Milwaukee—UP engine 2203 (on the left) would take night freight to Centralia while Milwaukee engine 1205 (on the right) would go to Tacoma.

Because of its important connections for the east, Number 696 was called the Harbor Highball, but was more affectionately known as the "Swamp Engine." I have never been able to find out for sure the origin of that name, but it undoubtedly has something to do with the perpetual dampness of the territory it traveled.

Sixth Avenue (later Titlow) Station, Tacoma, May 17, 1928.

The greatest frustration of taking railroad photographs as a hobby is to later realize that opportunities were missed—some subjects that once seemed so commonplace suddenly are gone. Fortunately, in some instances, someone else took pictures that have filled a missing gap in the record. James Fisher started work with the Northern Pacific as an office boy shortly before World War I, then served with the U.S. Army in France, and returned to the NP in 1918 for a fifty-year career in the Accounting Department. His hobby was photography and in 1927-28 this led to an assignment which I greatly envy. He was Traveling Joint Facilities Auditor and given the task of photographing every structure and much of the track in NP's joint territory (i.e., track shared by the NP with other roads—the GN, UP, etc.). And, I mean every structure—from the smallest outhouse to the largest depot!

The photos taken on the Seattle, Tacoma, and Idaho divisions were assembled in fourteen albums and included the history of the railroads as well as the buildings. It is an absolutely priceless collection! Before Fisher retired in the late 1950s, he was Supervisor of Joint Facility Accounts in St. Paul. Because of his expertise in railroad accounting, he was called back from retirement to testify at the Burlington Northern merger hearings in Washington, D.C., and New York City.

I am grateful to Fisher for taking this picture of the Sixth Avenue Station where I had one of my most memorable experiences as a relief agent. In July 1947, I was sent there to relieve Nell Bryan, who went on vacation, and it was a most inopportune time for a city boy like me to arrive on the scene. A hog farmer near Gig Harbor, who received his rail shipments at Sixth Avenue, had just collected a $50,000 claim from the Union Pacific for too many of his little pigs arriving comatose, or worse. And, wouldn't you know it—his first shipment after the claim arrived was while I was agent. I swear that every UP official from Omaha and all points west called me that day to be sure I would be on the scene to inspect the little critters and make certain they were in good health. The UP freight with the car of hogs was first reported due to arrive in the early afternoon, but as the day progressed, the arrival time became later and later.

Finally, at 11 p.m. on a pitch black night, the double-deck cattle car was set out on the house track, the farmer's truck backed up to it, a gang plank was put in place, and the door opened. Out swarmed a hoard of squealing little porkers and it was all I could do to count them, much less give them any kind of a physical examination. Fortunately, they all seemed to be alive. The next day the phone again rang continuously with UP officials wanting a report. I gave them all the same answer—they looked fine to me.

After all that, I don't know why I didn't take a picture of the depot. Maybe I just wanted to forget it.

Darrington Logger at Arlington, Washington, May 25, 1955.

A Seattle historian once wrote, "The day the Northern Pacific selected Tacoma as its Western Terminus was the day the Seattle spirit was born." To add insult to injury, the NP did everything it could to promote Tacoma and ignore Seattle.

Outraged Seattle citizens, led by Judge Thomas Burke and Daniel H. Gilman, adopted the philosophy "The Lord helps those who help themselves" and incorporated their own railroad on April 28, 1885. Named the Seattle, Lake Shore and Eastern, its goal was a direct connection to the East. One route was planned via Snoqualmie Pass to Spokane and Deadwood, Dakota Territory, and another to connect with the Canadian Pacific at Sumas.

Construction started on January 26, 1887, and rails had reached Sallal Prairie (North Bend) by the end of 1889 and Sumas in 1891. At the same time, construction was progressing west from Spokane and reached Davenport in 1889.

In 1891 events best described as ironic took place. The "Lake Shore" ran out of money, and the Northern Pacific was seeing the handwriting on the wall in regard to the approaching Great Northern. Realizing that Seattle could no longer be ignored, NP interests bought up the majority of SLS&E stock held by financial firms in the East. The name was changed to the Seattle and International and it was operated as an independent company until March 21, 1901, when it was formally sold to the Northern Pacific.

The Seattle and International started construction of the Darrington Branch and also purchased the Everett and Monte Cristo Railway. Other segments, too, of the NP's north end had their start as smart independent lines. The Wickersham to Bellingham Line began as the Bellingham Bay and Eastern, and the Lake Washington Belt Line from Black River to Woodinville was originally the Northern Pacific and Puget Sound Shore Railroad.

Incredible amounts of tonnage were hauled over the north end. Hot shots 675 and 676 ran between Auburn and Sumas to connect with the Canadian Pacific and British Columbia Electric. Monster trains were handled by the Auburn-Everett Turn that would often triple Maltby Hill even with the assistance of the helper engine based at Woodinville. On Mondays, the unique Banana Special ran to Sumas with bananas unloaded from a boat at Seattle and destined for the Canadian interior. Locals ran from Everett to Darrington, Everett to Bellingham, Woodinville to North Bend, Seattle to University, Auburn to Sedro Woolley, and Auburn to the Belt Line. Farther back in history, passenger trains were everywhere. At one time Canadian Pacific passenger trains went through to Seattle over the NP.

With the Burlington Northern merger, better grades on the former GN spelled instant doom for the NP's north end. Much of the NP track was removed. As a final bit of irony, the NP track is gone and all but forgotten between Interbay and Kenmore, but the names of the founders of the Seattle, Lake Shore and Eastern live on. The old right-of-way has been turned over to bicyclists, walkers, and joggers and is named the Burke Gilman Trail.

Oh, you can't scare me, I'm sticking to the union,
I'm sticking to the union, I'm sticking to the union.
Oh, you can't scare me, I'm sticking to the union,
I'm sticking to the union 'Till the day I die.
—From the song "Union Made" by Woody Guthrie.

Mostly, railroads have been remarkably free of major industrial strife for more than a century and a half. This is partially due to being an essential public utility, but also because the railways have been blessed with workers who are steady and frequently above average in intelligence and who have been guided by capable union leaders. There have been times, however, when railroaders felt justified in striking, and on two occasions this resulted in some of the most violent and bloody industrial upheavals the United States has ever seen.

In the 1870s, railroad companies had been making huge profits, but working conditions for the workers were miserable and the equipment and facilities were grossly unsafe. A final blow came in 1877 when the railroads announced a ten percent wage reduction for all workers earning more than $1 per day. Baltimore and Ohio firemen and brakemen refused to work and the walkout quickly spread to the rest of the system, then to the Pennsylvania Railroad and other roads in the East. The companies countered by urging state governors to call out the militia, and the governors in turn asked President Rutherford Hayes to add federal troops.

As a result, as many as ten-thousand militiamen, soldiers, and detectives were brought in to occupy and protect the Pennsylvania Railroad's facilities and tracks. Violence reached a peak in Pittsburgh when a thousand soldiers with artillery confronted fifteen thousand strikers, which included women among their ranks. At the height of the conflict, fires consumed railroad buildings and freight cars, and looting was prevalent. In the end, the unions suffered a bitter defeat; the final casualty toll showed that more than one hundred died and five times as many were wounded. Though the workers appeared to have been defeated, the strike of 1877 in fact was a major turning point for unions.

The Brotherhood of Locomotive Engineers had been founded in 1863, the Order of Railroad Conductors in 1868, and the Brotherhood of Locomotive Firemen and Enginemen in 1873. (The last of the "Big Four," the Brotherhood of Railroad Trainmen, would be organized after a strike in 1883.) Up to this time, the Brotherhoods had been largely fraternal organizations, but after 1877 they realized their goals could only be achieved through solidarity and collective bargaining. Thus, rising like a phoenix out of the 1877 troubles came the most successful labor unions in the country.

One more period of exceptional violence remained—the 1894 Pullman Strike in Chicago led by Eugene Debs and his American Railway Union, which had accomplished some of its early organizing in the Great Northern system and had gained popularity by gaining concessions from James J. Hill. After a long face-off between soldiers and workers, the Pullman Strike was broken and Debs ended up in jail, but long-range benefits resulted. The Brotherhoods now more than ever were convinced that their form of organization was the best for railroad workers. Debs became world famous and his counsel, Clarence Darrow, said "both sides recognized that Debs had been sent to jail because he had led a great fight to benefit the toilers and the poor." An ugly result of the Pullman Strike, however, was the blacklisting by management of all workers who had taken an active part.

By 1915, when this photo was taken, the bitterness between labor and owners apparently had subsided. Agent George Mounce and an unidentified telegrapher are proudly proclaiming that all the operators at Thorp belonged to the Order of Railroad Telegraphers. This was the first union to be organized after the combining of the "Big Four" in 1886, and it was followed by the Brotherhood of Maintenance of Way Employees in 1887, the Brotherhood of Railway Carmen in 1891, the Switchmen's Union of North America in 1894, the Brotherhood of Railway and Steamship Clerks, Freight Handlers, Express and Station Employees in 1898, and the Brotherhood of Railroad Signalmen in 1901. My union, the American Train Dispatchers Association, was founded in

Spokane in 1918. Other unions that strongly protected the rights of their members were the Railroad Yardmasters of America and the various shop craft unions.

In my time with the railroad, conditions have been dramatically improved through the efforts of the unions. When I first went to work in 1943, telegraphers worked seven days a week at straight time. There was no pay for "deadheading" and no away-from-home allowance; pay scales were under a dollar per hour. Engine crews worked sixteen hours a day in cabs that were like furnaces in the summer and deep freezers in the winter. Trainmen risked their lives riding in "crummies" that really deserved the nickname—they were little wooden cracker boxes that little resembled modern-day steel cabooses.

Technological innovations, led by the coming of the diesel locomotive, have caused a drastic decline in railroad employment and consequently a restructuring of the unions to maintain strength in numbers. In 1969, conductors, trainmen, firemen, switchmen, and yardmasters

joined together to form the United Transportation Union. The elimination of the Morse code for railroad communications and the closing of most of the small stations spelled doom for the ORT and the remaining operators now belong to the Clerks' Union, which has added "Airline" to its name.

With the heritage handed down from the valiant battlers of the past, unions still will succeed.

*Special train for "Seattle Times" paper carriers,
Steilacoom, Washington, 1953.*

Bitter winter weather means long hours of suffering for those whose jobs
are outdoors. I have always marveled at the endurance displayed by signal maintainers, carmen, switchmen, trainmen, and other "rails" who
keep the trains moving regardless of the weather.

My first effort at brewing a pot of coffee was at Stampede, out of
sympathy for the section men who were working around the clock
keeping the switches clean (no switch heaters in those days). I used
twice too much coffee, but anything hot was appreciated by those frozen bodies.

Even telegraph operators could have their moments of misery. I remember clinging to the top of the train order signal at Martin for an
hour in a raging snow storm trying to light the kerosene signal lamp,
and then being chastised by the dispatcher for being away from the
phone too long.

Outside of the railroad industry, mail carriers, service station workers,
and paperboys sacrifice personal comfort to serve us. *Seattle Times* carriers were given a little break from their winter drudgery with a trip to
Portland on an NP special train.

NP Class A-1 2626, "the Timken," at Auburn, May 12, 1953.

A Northern Pacific distribution of power bulletin dated March 1, 1933, contained this historic paragraph: "Sale of Timken locomotive No. 1111, to the Northern Pacific having been consummated, it has been classified as A-1, number changed to 2626, and locomotive assigned to the Tacoma Division."

The Timken Roller Bearing Company had been trying unsuccessfully to sell the railroads on the idea of using roller bearings instead of the conventional friction bearings on steam locomotives. Finally in 1929, Timken President T.V. Buckwalter decided that the only way to prove their concept was correct would be to build a demonstration engine of their own. The American Locomotive Company was given the order to build a 4-8-4 completely equipped with roller bearings and designed for both freight and passenger service. In April 1930, this masterpiece of locomotive technology rolled out of Alco's Schenectady plant. It was given the number TRBX 1111 and naturally christened The Four Aces. The usual numbers on the side of the headlight were replaced by a heart, diamond, spade, and club.

For the next two years, the 1111 was given every grueling test imaginable in both freight and passenger service on fourteen different railroads and passed them all with flying colors. Much publicity appeared in the nation's newspapers during the testing, especially photographs of three young women pulling this giant machine with a rope attached to the pilot, a feat impossible with friction bearings. The final phase of the testing was conducted over the entire Northern Pacific system, and at the conclusion the NP successfully negotiated its purchase.

The 1111 was redesignated the 2626, but the name Timken was lettered under the cab number, and "All Journals Equipped with Timken Roller Bearings" was emblazoned under the Northern Pacific name on the tender. From then on she was virtually always referred to as "the Timken" and seldom by number, except in formal train orders and messages.

Thousands of words were written and many tales have been told about the Timken, but two of my favorite anecdotes appeared in articles written by my good friends Ron Nixon and Max "Mickey" King. In the February 2, 1958, *Spokane Spokesman-Review*, in an article titled "Four Aces Set Records as It Rolled," Ron related the following true tale of an incident during the testing on the NP:

One evening while 1111 was hauling the *North Coast Limited*, engineer Jimmy Jones was delayed at Whitehall, Mont., for "inspection." Traveling late, Jimmy whooped her up on the level, tangent track between Sappington and Three Forks. Arriving at Livingston on time, Jimmy was asked about the delay at Whitehall. He replied, "Well, it's like this. I wanted to get behind schedule so as to beat that doggone record on the Pennsy." He beat it all right—88 miles per hour by the tape in the dynamometer car!

One of Mickey's many great stories on local railroading history was entitled "Old 2626 . . . She Was the Greatest," which appeared in the *Tacoma News Tribune* on November 12, 1967. He presented the history of the Timken and then gave a vivid account of "his first chance at the Timken's throttle." He was called for train 402, the Seattle to Portland *Owl* with engine 2626, twenty-three cars, and conductor Gus Barnett. To quote from the story:

Observing the consist of our train, I was aware that any one of the 2600's would be in trouble with a train of this magnitude. I said, "Gus, with a drag like this, what's our chance of pulling into Portland on time?" Said Gus: "Mickey, you forgot you got the Timken!" (The Timken had pulled him before.) "When you get the sign, you get that throttle open and don't look back, because we trainmen will be on, and then do a hundred miles an hour between stations if you can." Gus winked at me and said, "See you on time in Portland! This train is little more or less than a glorified freight train, but we want her on time and you can do it."

Max went on to relate the difficulties of that run—the exceptionally heavy train, the many station stops, and switching more cars in at Tacoma that caused them to be up to an hour late at one point. I can see the smile on Mickey's face as he wrote the last paragraph:

We rolled down to the Portland station and cut loose from the train where I inspected the engine. The fireman and myself then walked up to the telegraph office, where I registered in. On the register I found a duplicate copy of the conductor's delay report. In bold hand he had written: "On time—also handled the train very nicely. Gus Barnett."

The Grays Harbor and Bremerton-Bangor branches were a jigsaw puzzle of short line logging roads that failed, Northern Pacific subsidiaries, and finally, as a result of World War II, a segment built by the U.S. government. Northern Pacific interests incorporated the Tacoma, Olympia and Gray's Harbor Railroad which started operating from Centralia to Elma on May 1, 1891. (A portion of this line was acquired from a logging road with the grandiose name of Tacoma, Olympia and Chehalis Valley Railroad.) At the same time, track was being laid from Lakeview to Gate, which was finished on August 10, 1891.

The next piece of the puzzle was another logging road—the Puget Sound and Gray's Harbor—built from Kamilche to Montesano in 1887-89. This railway was purchased by the Tacoma, Olympia and Gray's Harbor, which then finished the line from Montesano to Ocosta in 1892 only to be absorbed shortly thereafter by another NP subsidiary—the United Railroads of Washington.

Finally, in 1898, the NP came out of the closet and formally purchased the United Railroads. Construction was completed from Aberdeen to Hoquiam to Moclips in 1905.

Without the coming of World War II, the line constructed from Stimson to Shelton in 1925 (over the grade of the old Port Blakely Mill logging railroad) would have wrapped up railway building in this part of the state. But with a war raging in the Pacific, the government felt it urgent not only to provide direct rail service to the Bremerton Navy Yard, but also to eliminate the movement of high explosives on barges across the sound. Construction was started on the government line from Shelton to Bangor-Bremerton early in 1944 and it was turned over to the Northern Pacific for contract operations on April 10, 1945. The new line was well equipped to handle wartime traffic. In addition to the facilities opened at Bangor and Bremerton there were telegraph offices at Bremerton Jct. and NAD Jct. (Naval Ammunition Depot). Through trains were handled by NP crews and power. The Navy, however, ran its own trains from Bangor to NAD Jct., thence on its private trackage to the magazine on Ostrich Bay, about four miles northwest of Bremerton. Class Z-3 Mallet steam engines, recently bumped off the Cascade mountain main line by new diesel engines, were assigned to the Bremerton Branch to handle the heavy tonnage over the steep grades.

Russ Wiecking, agent at Bangor from 1946 until 1959, remembered the immense volume of high explosives arriving on as many as four trains a day. A particularly busy one-week period brought in the incredible total of $14,000,000 in freight bills and Russ was hard-pressed to convince the St. Paul accounting office that a one-man branch line station could do this much business.

Earl Foss, Bremerton agent from 1961 until the station closed in 1982, recalled rare passenger train movements, notably a special with sailors of the Argentine navy sent to Bremerton to man one of their ships that had undergone repairs. When this train tried to negotiate the sharp curves inside the Navy base with the eighty-five foot Pullmans, the generator belts snapped one by one with a sound like gunfire.

Dick Leary never forgot one agonizing day of dispatching this territory, when a twenty car Navy dependents' special was run from Bremerton to take the families of the sailors on an aircraft carrier to their new home in Florida. When the complex train orders had finally been issued, Dick mopped the sweat from his brow and tipped over his ink bottle on the train sheet, obliterating the train movement records in his territory for the entire day.

During the Viet Nam conflict, rail traffic to Bangor was especially heavy with ninety-car trains of bombs an almost daily occurrence. The record for a train with the most cars, 121, loaded with bombs is held jointly by engineers Joe LaPorte and Carl Peterson. Joe handled this monster train with seven diesel units from Centralia to Bayshore, where Carl took over for the remainder of the run to Bangor. As the train was departing Bayshore, Joe observed a broken wheel on one of the bomb cars, radioed the news to Carl, and the car was set out. Joe's alertness possibly saved a derailment to end all derailments, and he received a letter of commendation from Superintendent John Hertog.

Great Northern 2586, Class S-2, at Auburn on the "Oriental Limited," May 30, 1948.

Yes, Virginia, there was a Great Northern. Someone reading this book who is not familiar with railroading history might get the impression that the Northern Pacific was the only railroad in the Northwest prior to the Burlington merger, which took in both lines. This is mainly because ninety percent of my photo collection relates to the NP.

Even before starting work in 1943, I had developed a fierce loyalty to the Northern Pacific and looked upon any competitor, especially the Great Northern with its mountain goat symbol, as the "enemy." Consequently I felt it would be akin to treason to photograph anything but the NP. Probably the reason I deviated from this narrow-minded philosophy and photographed the 2586 was because it was detouring over the NP when the GN main line was blocked. l shudder now to think of the golden photographic opportunities I passed by, especially when working as telegrapher at Lowell, where the giant GN Mallet engines would stop in front of the depot when making their pick-up. My friend and ace railroad photographer Warren McGee often scolded me for not photographing everything on rails, but I failed to heed his advice, much to my everlasting regret.

I guess we all mellow with age and some of my best railroad friendships have come from the ranks of the former enemy. At the risk of omitting someone important, I will mention a few of these ex-"billy goats." When I was night chief dispatcher in Tacoma, my counterpart in Seattle was Verle Kildee, a real gentleman and an extremely competent "rail." Same words apply to Charlie Duffy, who was the night diesel controller in St. Paul for the west end. It was a real pleasure to work with these two, and also Seattle Chief Dispatcher Ed Khatain and his assistant, Fred Frahm. Three Seattle dispatchers that I got to know had the unique experience of working for both the NP and the GN. Bert Giles started with the NP as an operator in the Tacoma area, but soon resigned and went with the GN at Whitefish, Montana. Arnold MacFarland was GN agent at Merritt before starting with the NP at Stampede. My fellow historian, Dave Sprau, was dispatching for the NP at Tacoma in 1969 when he heard the GN was hiring firemen. Visualizing himself as a second Casey Jones, he took advantage of this opportunity, but soon decided dispatching was best after all and transferred to the GN dispatchers' office in Seattle. Dale Voss made a similar move from NP operator to GN fireman (and later became a BN engineer).

The first superintendent of the Pacific Division of the BN, Tom Mackenroth, was from the GN as was the assistant superintendent at Tacoma, Dick Tanguy, who was familiar to all of us from his days as a conductor on the south end GN 672 trains.

My first "boss" when I went to the Seattle Transportation office was longtime GN official Deane Carlson, and I worked at the same desk with Marty Johnson from the GN, who never admitted that the NP was anything more than a streak of rust.

Around Tacoma, Paul Meyers symbolized the Great Northern and was affectionately known by his thousands of friends as the "old goat." Barb Johnson, Gerry Turner, and Jim Howard gave the GN touch to the Tacoma freight and yard offices. Milt Whitsell was terminal manager. Jake Wahl was OS&D claim inspector for the Great Northern, and Ed Adams retired from BN Safety and Rules after a long GN career.

The GN's 2586 was built by the Baldwin Locomotive Works in March 1930. Its notable features were the unusually high eighty-inch drivers, designed for speed, and the massive air pumps mounted on the front of the boiler. It must have been a truly impressive sight wheeling the *Empire Builder* at eighty miles per hour across the prairies. Almost as impressive as my beloved NP 2600s.

House at Lester, Washington, built by mill owner E.G. Morgan.

There's E.G. Morgan going home
He is as good as gold
A finer man where'er you roam
You never will behold,
The call-boy's coming for you dad,
I guess it's for Number 2.
There's Keywood coming down the hill
He helped the Local's crew.
Heater's throwing of the switch
To let them in the yard;
While fireman Saunders
keeps a watch
That cows don't get hit hard . . .

This excerpt from the poem "Lester" by John E. Brown mentions the two owners of this magnificent home. E.G. Morgan was a virtual lumber baron with mills and logging camps at Lester, and at Weston on the old line five miles east of Lester and at Nagrom (Morgan spelled backwards) six miles west of Lester. His principal residence was in Seattle, and he built this house at Lester as a summer home. By the 1920s, the railroad was gone from Weston, his two mills at Lester had burned, and consequently his operations were centered at Nagrom, which by then was a community rivaling Lester in size. There were enough Morgan employees to field two baseball teams, and he had built his own railroad up Smay Creek to bring logs down to the mill. As he divided his time between Nagrom and Seattle, Morgan no longer had much use for his Lester home.

Northern Pacific engineer Herbert "Pop" Saunders was in the Lester helper engine service at the time and raised dairy cows as a sideline. He supplied the Morgan logging camps with milk, but with the mill fires and other financial setbacks, the milk bills went unpaid. In reaching a settlement, the Morgan house became the Saunders house. It would have been a near mansion in a large city, and for a small village like Lester it was a truly unique place for the seven Saunders children— Bill, Emily, Helen, Bertram (Bud), Frances, Dorothy, and Margaret (Mickey) to spend their childhood. They well remember the luxurious interior and the fine furniture the Morgans had left behind. The combination dining room-library had a giant table with lions' heads carved in the legs, and the floors were covered with oriental rugs. The bedrooms were furnished with marble-top dressers and had stained glass windows. A hand-carved mahogany staircase made a super slide for the kids. The kitchen was a separate building attached to the main house and had three buffet cupboards stocked with hand painted china.

Then in the early 1930s came a heart breaking tragedy. The coal stove overheated while the family was away and the house burned to the ground.

Accompanied by Helen Saunders Steele and veteran mountain track supervisor Matt Fioretti, I visited the site of the Saunders house. Clearly visible were the sidewalks and the remains of the once beautiful rock gardens. Visiting Lester and remembering its glorious days of railroading and logging is a bittersweet experience.

Thanks to former Lester Station Agent Ruth Trueblood Eckes for allowing me to make a copy of this picture. It is one of a set of old Lester photos given to her by old-time storekeeper Ed Hocking when he was closing out his business.

NP 1070, Class L-9 switch engine at Tacoma, June 11, 1954.

Tacoma's most elegant hotel from the time it was built in 1884 until destroyed by fire in October 1935 was the Tacoma, located at 9th and A Streets on the bluffs above the Northern Pacific tracks. In spring 1910, to further enhance its reputation as Tacoma's premier establishment, the hotel opened an outdoor dining area. An unexpected problem arose from the NP's Moon Yard below that resulted in the following letter being written by the hotel's manager to NP Superintendent W.C. Albee:

> Your yardmen must have guessed that we were attempting to start our outdoor business for they have kept us enveloped in black smoke and sulpherous fumes. At the time I am writing this, 8:30 p.m., for two or three blocks around here, it is difficult to breathe and if the ante room to Hell is anything worse than the N.P. gives us, God help the poor wretches who go there. I have had to have the doors and windows closed, but even so, the guests and help are busy coughing their hearts out.
>
> If I had the power I wouldn't wish anything worse for you than to make you take about two hours of your own medicine. Perhaps then you wouldn't so carefully keep three or four engines belching out their abominations below.
>
> Frankly, it strikes me as an outrage that the N.P. should be willing to perpetrate this sort of thing at the expense of innocent outsiders.

An innocent participant in this little drama was the 1070 or some of her sister L-9s who for many years faithfully served the switching needs of Tacoma's many industries.

The 1070 retains a quality that eluded most other NP steam locomotives—she is a survivor. She was purchased by the Lake Whatcom Scenic Railway and harnessed to pull a tourist train on the former Bellingham Branch of the Northern Pacific, starting at Wickersham and running 3 1/2 miles each way. I have accompanied members of the Northern Pacific Historical Society to Wickersham and it was truly thrilling to see the 1070 shining like she was fresh out of the South Tacoma Shops, pulling three NP passenger cars that look just as they did in the good old days.

NP Auburn to Tacoma Transfer crossing Stuck River bridge, March 3, 1952.

Even more incredible than the life and death of two small but busy stations, Easton and Kanaskat, was the demise of much larger and busier "valley" stations—Puyallup, Sumner, Auburn, and Kent. In the 1940s, when I was working as a relief operator, it required no less than forty years seniority to hold a regular day position as agent or operator at one of these stations. Not only were they good places to live, as compared to many of the remote and isolated stations, but the agents enjoyed a lucrative commission on Railway Express, received and forwarded, and the day operators collected a similar commission on the substantial Western Union business. (Western Washington Fair week was a real bonanza for the agent at Puyallup, with many of the exhibits arriving by express.) Each of these stations had clerks as well as operators to handle the heavy volume of express, freight, and passenger business.

I particularly remember working the entire summer of 1946 on second trick at Puyallup. I had been struggling to master Morse Code and it was a matter of "sink or swim" when copying from the highly proficient and somewhat egotistical Western Union operators, who refused to slow down for "lids" like me. It was an excellent way to learn in a hurry. Other memories of Puyallup include Hoquiam to Seattle passenger train Number 423 stopping for up to thirty minutes while express shipments of blueberries and Venetian blinds were being loaded. Likewise, mail sacks from the midnight *Owl* Number 402 filled several baggage trucks to overflowing. Of course the biggest loss in the valley resulting from the Burlington Northern merger was the giant freight yard and roundhouse facility at Auburn.

In the days of the Northern Pacific, westbound transcontinental freight trains terminated at Auburn and cars for Tacoma and Seattle went forward on "transfers" such as the train pictured here. Much of the acreage in the valley has been transformed from farms to industrial use, and there is still much railroad activity in the Kent-Orillia industrial complex, but customers who once had friendly railroad folk right in town to deal with must now do business by phone with Tacoma or Seattle.

All of this brings to mind several quotations. A pre-merger brochure issued by the railroads said: "A dismaying and continuing downward trend in employment has seen jobs of the four railroads decline by more than 13,000 in the past four years. The progressive, dynamic new company will not only reverse this trend and create new jobs but also will bring new prosperity to railroad communities."

NP-BN President Louis Menk's comment is also well remembered: "There will always be an Auburn."

NP Conductor Warren McGee, while heading the Livingston Anti-Merger Committee, said over and over: "The managers of today cannot speak for the managers of tomorrow." His prophetic words fell on too many deaf ears.

Temporary depot at Kanaskat, March 19, 1944.

Kanaskat is another station on the NP First Subdivision that once was the center of so much activity that it now is hard to believe that nothing is left. Westbound local trains would come into town with one-hundred cars of logs picked up at Maywood, Humphrey, and Eagle Gorge, and would wait until the waybills for all these cars were made. It was also necessary to make interchange reports showing empties to, and loads from, the logging railroads connecting with the NP. A local was based at Kanaskat that went to Enumclaw in the morning to bring loads of lumber back from Enumclaw and Palmer and coal from Bayne to be picked up by eastbound trains. In the afternoon, the local went north from Kanaskat to pick up logs at Selleck and coal at Durham. When all of the branch line loads were assembled at Kanaskat, the local would push them over the scales while the operator weighed them. All of this clerical work, together with Kanaskat being a key train order station, made it one of the busiest telegrapher jobs I ever worked.

For years Kanaskat had one of the classic NP two-story wooden depots, but in 1943 one of my fellow operators working third trick stoked too much coal in the big old heating stove and dozed off. The stovepipe turned red hot all the way to the ceiling, and the building caught fire and burned to the ground. While an elegant new brick depot was being constructed, a boxcar was pressed into temporary service as a station. Standing in the doorway is Agent Stan Edwall and barely visible at his side is night operator Ruth Trueblood Eckes' German shepherd dog. The boxcar actually was a convenient depot to work in as, from a swivel chair, all of the station supplies were within easy reach.

The new brick depot had a short life as a railroad station as the tracks were moved away from it with the Eagle Gorge line change. The federal government constructed a duplicate brick depot on the new line. Ernie Harrison bought the original brick depot at the time of the line change (June 1959), but later sold it back to the NP Timber Department, which used it as an office before moving to Enumclaw. Later it was rented for office space by a contractor. The new depot on the present line was last used as office and supply room for the section foreman, but when all activity ceased, it was boarded up.

NP 5138, Class Z-8, at the Easton, Washington, coal dock, July 1, 1944.

When this photo was taken, Tacoma Division's Auburn to Yakima First Subdivision (The Mountain) was one of the Northern Pacific's most dynamic segments. There were four regular passenger trains each way (the *North Coast Limited* was running two sections), frequent troop trains and, with World War II at its peak, the freight traffic was almost overwhelming.

The busiest spot on this busy piece of railroad was Easton. All westbound trains headed for the Cascade Range stopped at Easton for their helper engines, usually two on each freight train and one or two on passenger trains. And to further complicate the operation, most freight trains changed their road engine at Easton.

In 1935 the Northern Pacific had launched a program of purchasing steam locomotives that were capable of both high speed and heavy tonnage. The design selected was a simple articulated 4-6-6-4 "Challenger" type numbered in the 5100 series, with the initial order designated Class Z-6 and later orders Z-7 and Z-8. NP was a pioneer in adopting this style of locomotive, which was to later become the most widely used modern articulated. They were a marvelous piece of machinery, but had one drawback as far as this part of the railroad was concerned—they were too big to go through the ancient Stampede Tunnel. Actually, in 1939, test runs were made with the 5117 going through to Auburn, but the temperature in the cab rose to a suffocating 130 degrees shortly after entering the tunnel, and there was fear that the powerful exhaust blast from the smokestack would crumble the tunnel ceiling. Therefore, the 5100s brought trains as far west as Easton and then were traded off for venerable, almost worn-out Z-3 Mallets for the rest of the run to Auburn.

NP was working on interesting solutions to this problem—electrification, cab-in-front steam locomotives, digging a lower, longer tunnel, enlarging the Stampede Tunnel, to name a few—but suddenly the ultimate solution, the diesel locomotive, burst upon the scene. This sealed the doom of steam engines and stations like Easton, as well as revolutionizing railroading as a whole.

A magnificent book has been published on NP history in general and the "superpower" Yellowstones, Northerns, and Challengers in particular. The title is *Northern Pacific Railway Supersteam Era, 1925–1945,* by co-authors Robert L. Frey and Lorenz P. Schrenk, who did incredibly detailed and well written research on the development and performance of these incomparable engines.

GN electric 5019 at Wenatchee, Washington, May 25, 1952.

The GN's Walt Grecula went railroading the same year (1943) as I did. Walt grew up in Hibbing, Minnesota, the "iron ore capital of the world," and had an early railroading connection as his father was a locomotive engineer on a switch engine for the Scranton mine. Walt became fascinated with electricity at an early age and after high school studied electricity at the Dunwoody Institute in Minneapolis. When he finished this course, he was hired by the GN Lines East electrical department and assigned to the Allouez ore docks installing conduits for lights and power. This proved to be an excellent way to learn the trade, and after a year and a half, Walt was transferred to an electrical construction crew at Whitefish, Montana. Then, in 1950, he was made electrical foreman with headquarters at Great Falls, and the next two years were spent stringing power lines and wiring buildings at Havre, Shelby, Butte, Helena, and other stations as far east as Williston, North Dakota.

In 1952 Walt became assistant to the electrical supervisor and electrical engineer in Seattle and was their "trouble shooter" for problems on the line. From 1956 to 1966, he returned to St. Paul as electrical supervisor and then came back to Seattle as assistant electrical engineer until the merger, when he was promoted to electrical engineer for the Seattle Region of the Burlington Northern, retiring in 1984.

Here is a photo of GN 5019, although Walt Grecula's department was not involved with the locomotives or electrified trackage as they belonged to the Mechanical Department. The Great Northern installed a short 2-1/2 mile electrified section in 1909 through the old, high-elevation Cascade Tunnel so that electric locomotives could pull steam engines and their trains through the "hole" with no smoke. When the new, eight-mile tunnel was opened in 1929, steam engines were cut off and replaced by electrics at Wenatchee, going west, and Skykomish, going east. In 1955, with the steam engines gone, GN decided not to renew the electricity contract with Puget Sound Power, and instead installed a ventilating system so that the diesel engines could run through the tunnel. This required electrically operated doors at the east portal and Walt Grecula spent countless hours on the doors, the fan motors, and their problems.

The 5019 was the newest, largest, and most powerful of the GN electrics. Once, when I was making a trip to Spokane, I decided to take the *Oriental Limited* and was visiting with King Street operator Bill Eldridge before departure time. When the engineer walked in to register, Bill said, "this dispatcher wants to ride in the engine with you," and the Hoghead said, "OK." I vividly remember the engine change at Skykomish and the massive size of the 5019 which was our replacement electric. After climbing the long ladder to the cab door, there was a stairway inside to get to the seat. The electrics were not loud and flamboyant like a steam engine, but they had their own unique personality.

Jim and Tim Fredrickson aboard NP's "Mainstreeter," August 11, 1959.

Recounting a 1959 vacation provides a good glimpse of the kind of passenger train service that once was available on our railroads.

My sons and I left Spokane on NP's *Mainstreeter* for a daylight trip through some of the most beautiful scenery anywhere—mile after mile along Lake Pend Oreille and the Clark Fork River of northern Idaho and western Montana. We then left the NP at Butte, Montana, and boarded the UP's *Butte Special* for an overnight ride to Salt Lake City. From there we had a vista-dome view of Royal Gorge and the Colorado Rockies on the Denver and Rio Grande Western's *Royal Gorge,* getting off at Pueblo, Colorado, to see the Indian cliff dwellings. Next it was the Missouri Pacific's *Colorado Eagle* to Colorado Springs where we took the Manito and Pike's Peak Railway cog train to the summit of Pikes Peak. Then to Denver on the Santa Fe and home again on the Union Pacific's *Portland Rose.* It was a magnificent way to see what the West was really like as opposed to a view from 39,000 feet in the air!

The photo shows Jim and Tim concentrating on a game of cards in the *Mainstreeter's* holiday lounge car, correctly described by the NP as being luxurious. A brochure gave a detailed description of the car:

> The rich appointments include fluorescent lighting, deep pile carpeting and African cherry wood paneling. Gold and black colors predominate. Window shades and draperies are done in gold, as are the parlor chairs and the lounge sofas. Etchings of

Northern Pacific's "Gold Spike" locomotive and other engines, and a replica of a pioneer locomotive headlight are part of the decorative scheme [the photo shows these features]. Planters with greenery also add an interesting touch in the lounge.

I have no complaints about AMTRAK's present-day passenger cars, as they are extremely quiet and comfortable. What is missing is the individual treatment each railroad in days past applied to its equipment.

Station at Woodland, Washington, March 25, 1944.

NP depots were built to standard plans and the depot at Woodland was almost identical to innumerable small town stations throughout the system. The ground floor had an office room with a bay window for the telegrapher's desk, so that approaching trains could easily be seen, and a large freight room for the safekeeping of freight and express. In those days, small shipments went by Railway Express and larger packages were sent by the railroad's Less Than Carload (LCL) service. The entire system had local train service and each local had a "peddler" car for the LCL business. For whatever reason, the passion for hurrying had not yet become an integral part of the American way of life.

The upper floor of these stations contained the living quarters for the agent and his family. Telegrapher and dispatcher Jimmie Wyse grew up in the depots at Adna and Raymond (both on the South Bend Branch) where his father was agent. The standard floor plan called for a living room, kitchen, one bedroom, and a small bathroom. (Part of the plumbing was housed in a small structure outside.) With three children in the family, Wyse's father prevailed upon the railroad to build a 10x10 foot bedroom over the high-ceilinged freight room at Adna so that the three children would have a place to sleep. The crowded conditions were not ideal, but the small-town agent was always one of the most respected members of the community and it was a highly satisfying profession.

Actually, Woodland Station was little more than a "flag stop" when I was there. In 1913, however, when passenger trains were the only way to go, fifteen trains made regular stops here (counting both directions), four stopped when flagged, and only three "limiteds" went by without stopping. When I worked there in 1944, four trains made regular stops and four roared by without halting.

NP Number 408 at Woodland, March 25, 1944.

After returning to Tacoma from working at Woodland, I printed the photos I had taken. When I showed a picture of Train Number 408 to the local safety supervisor, he was impressed and submitted it to the Northern Pacific's *Tell Tale*, a monthly publication for employees. He wrote a somewhat exaggerated story to go with the picture, and this is what it said:

Railroader Makes Photography a Hobby—
Jimmy Fredrickson Photos Crack Seattle-Portland Passenger Train No. 408 at 60 Miles Per Hour

Jimmy Fredrickson, Age 17, Senior in Stadium High School, Tacoma, whose hobby is photography, has centered on railroad locomotives. He has several hundred pictures of Northern Pacific Locomotives in use on the system west of Missoula. He began this hobby several years ago and his interest in locomotives led to his going to work as call boy at Tacoma in April 1943. In November 1943 he started to work as an Extra Telegrapher, working week-ends, and is at present so engaged. He is probably the youngest railroad telegrapher on the system and possibly in the nation.

The picture of Train No. #408, Engine 2610, taken at Woodland, Washington, while train was traveling 60 miles per hour, is typical of his collection. This is a remarkable photo as you will note the train definitely appears to be standing still. To get this result he used a shutter speed of 1/550 of a second with lens opening at F.8. He has a Graflex camera, 2-1/4 x 3-1/4, with highest speed 1/1000 of a second.

Jimmy has a most interesting hobby, one which requires a great deal of patience and attendance to details. In following his hobby, Jimmy will get a lot of training to assist him in handling his position as operator—one of the most important railroad jobs in the handling of safe, fast, dependable transportation.

I start to say, "it seems like only yesterday," but actually it seems more like a thousand years ago. Footnote: The one part of this little story that is not exaggerated and probably underestimated is the speed of the train. In conversations with veteran steam engineers Hugh Carroll, Carl France, Ken Leavens, Pat Loughlin, and Don Wilson, they all said they had gone well over 80 mph in a 2600 class engine. I have heard estimates as high as 110 mph. The speedometer only went as far as 80, and when they were late and on straight track, the needle would be against the peg. As Pat said, "We went fast enough to put fingerprints on the arm rest."

NP Decapod locomotive 500 at Stampede Pass in 1887.

With mushrooming modern transportation systems and technology—jet airlines, freeways, dieselized and computerized railroads—one of the most significant dates in the history of the Northwest is fading into oblivion, and only a little over a century after it occurred. On June 1, 1887, the last spike was driven at the summit of the Stampede switchback and for the first time it was possible to cross the Cascade Range without going on foot, horseback, or wagon. The first train over the mountains arrived in Tacoma on June 6 and in essence was a test run with two locomotives, a baggage car, coach, and caboose, with Assistant General Manager J.M. Buckley (for whom the town of Buckley was named) aboard. With the test train proving to be a success, a second train ran the next day with a parlor car carrying NP director and former president Charles B. Wright for a triumphal arrival in Tacoma. Regularly scheduled trains commenced operating on July 3, and the Fourth of July marked the beginning of a gigantic three-day civic celebration sponsored by Tacoma.

Stampede Pass was discovered in March 1881 by NP Assistant Civil Engineer Virgil Bogue, who had hoped the pass would be named after him. Instead, NP officials named it Garfield Pass in honor of the recently assassinated U.S. president, but that name was short lived. Bogue had become dissatisfied with his trail-cutting crew at the summit and put a notorious "slave driver" in charge as foreman to stimulate faster progress. This move backfired as all but one of the men rebelled against the new boss and took off for Tacoma. The one remaining cutter, Johnny Bradley of Puyallup, nailed a board to a tree with "Stampede Camp" written on it and the designation has remained ever since.

Nelson Bennett was awarded the contract to build the line from Yakima to Tacoma (including a 9,850 feet tunnel "through the north shoulder of Mount Rainier") with a stipulation that the job be finished by May 22, 1888. It was a Herculean task. They had only vague pack trails to follow and nature threw all of her arsenal of weapons at them—mud, rain, snow, and ice during an incredibly severe winter. Naturally, it was difficult to keep men on the job under these conditions. Bennett's brother, Sidney, who was directing the work, remarked that he needed three crews at all times, "one coming, one drilling, one quitting."

With the slow progress and Congress talking about rescinding unearned land grants, the Northern Pacific decided in mid-1886 to build a temporary switchback line over the summit of the pass so that trains could commence operating before the tunnel was finished. This zigzag line up the face of the mountain, with a maximum grade of 5.6 per cent, was another monumental job requiring 2,000 men to build thirty-two trestles and shovel snowdrifts up to fifteen feet high.

To battle this severe grade, the NP ordered the two largest locomotives that had been built up to that time. They were purchased from the Baldwin Locomotive Works in 1886, numbered 500 and 501, and given the name Decapod because of their ten driving wheels. The switchback trains were limited to five cars with the 500 on one end facing one direction and the 501 on the other end facing in the opposite direction. Each leg of the switchback was a dead end track, thus there always was an engine going forward while the train zigzagged on the mountain. Tacoma adopted the Decapods as a symbol of civic pride.

The Bennett brothers completed the Stampede Tunnel seven days before the deadline—May 14, 1888. With the tunnel open, the switchback operation was finished and the Decapods' glory days quickly faded. They had many mechanical problems and were probably the most disappointing engines the NP ever ordered. The Decapods managed to fulfill their switchback assignment, but once that was over they were relegated to branch line and switch jobs until scrapped in the early 1930s.

Train ferry "Tacoma" on the Columbia River, 1907.

Towering mountain ranges were not the only obstacles facing the intrepid builders of the Northern Pacific over a century ago. Bridging broad, swift rivers was a costly, time-consuming process that brought about unique solutions for pushing train service through. No doubt the most unusual feat was laying track across the frozen Missouri River between Bismarck and Mandan, North Dakota, during the winters of 1879-82. After the ice broke up in the springtime, a ferry carried trains across the river during the warm months of the year. Eventually, a bridge was erected. Another train ferry, the *Frederick T. Billings*, was used in the 1880s when a bridge was being constructed over the mouth of the Snake River at Ainsworth, Washington, followed by another nearby bridge over the Columbia River between Pasco and Kennewick. These were relatively short-term operations during times when the bridges were under construction.

West of the Cascades, the broad, deep course of the lower Columbia River proved to be a special challenge. The company simply did not have the funds or resources to erect a bridge of the magnitude needed to cross the vast stream. The original NP line from Kalama, Washington, to Tacoma was completed in 1873, and track from Portland to Hunters Landing, Oregon, was finished in 1883, leaving about three miles of river floodplain separating the two segments. Giant problems produce giant solutions and the Northern Pacific ordered the construction of a ferry (it would be the second largest in the world at that time) for the staggering price of $400,000. The vessel was constructed in Wilmington, Delaware, then taken apart into 57,159 pieces and shipped around Cape Horn on the sailing vessel *Tillie Starbuck*. It was reassembled in Portland at the foot of Hall Street and launched in the Willamette River on May 17, 1884. It was a magnificent vessel—338 feet long and seventy-six feet wide, with twenty-nine feet high side paddles powered by a pair of five-hundred horsepower steam engines. The ferry had room for three sets of tracks with a capacity to hold two locomotives and fifteen passenger cars or twenty-three freight cars.

This great ferry originally was christened *Kalama*, but later its name was changed to *Tacoma*. Her maiden run from Kalama to Hunters Landing occurred on July 23, 1884, and regular runs began on October 9. In 1890 the track on the Oregon side was extended two miles from Hunters to Goble, and the ferry landing slip was moved to the new end of track. This cut the river distance down to a mile and three-quarters, which the *Tacoma* crossed in twenty minutes. NP timetables indicate that trains required only forty minutes for loading, crossing, and unloading. It appears to have been a remarkably smooth process—so efficient, in fact, that the operation continued for twenty-four years. In 1908 the Columbia finally was bridged at Vancouver. The *Tacoma* made her last NP run on December 25, 1908, and later was sold to the Milwaukee Road, which converted the vessel into a barge.

Earliest known picture of a Northern Pacific train in western Washington, taken at Kalama in 1872 by Oliver Dennie, a Portland photographer.

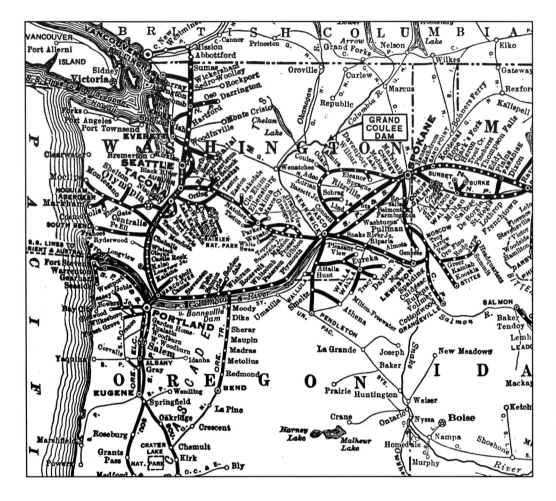

Map from a passenger train schedule, Winter 1937-38.

NP's pride in their high-powered locomotives is evident in this advertisement from the Seattle Times, *March 5, 1929. In railroad nomenclature an engineer was known as a "hoghead." One is depicted here with a steady hand on the throttle and a keen eye on the track ahead.*

Engineering *your* Comfort

By JOE DULIN, Engineer
"North Coast Limited"

"Talk about giants! This engine on Number 2 ('North Coast Limited') is a brute for power, yet sensitive as a fine auto. You've got to handle the air and throttle just right if you're going to have her stop and start 'easy like.'

"When we're pulling Number 2 we always think of the folks back there in the sleepers and diner—they must ride smooth. Our roadbed is a big help—you can't make time and keep your cars rolling smoothly unless you've got good ballast underneath.

"I've heard lots of passengers talking about the fine trip they had and how well they slept on Number 2. It's easy to keep the coffee from spilling on a dining car table if you know your engine and handle her right."

The Northern Pacific's new giant locomotives—104 feet long—provide a smooth flow of mighty power that makes for unusual comfort.

Travel—
"**North Coast Limited**"
Extra Comforts—No Extra Fare
68 Hours of Travel Luxury to Chicago
Leaves Seattle 11:00 a. m. daily

May we help you plan your next trip? Tickets delivered to your home or office.

N. J. HEUCHAN, *General Agent;* ORVILLE NEER, *City Passenger Agent*
Ticket Office: 1407 Fourth Avenue; ELliott 5560

Northern Pacific Railway
"First of the Northern Transcontinentals"

The NP was the first transcontinental railroad to provide passenger service to Yellowstone National Park. It was such a lucrative venture that the NP added the tag "Yellowstone Park Line" to the Monad logo.

Sleeping cars on the North Coast Limited *were named after famous Northwest and Plains Indian leaders. Biographical descriptions of the chiefs were presented in this informative brochure.*

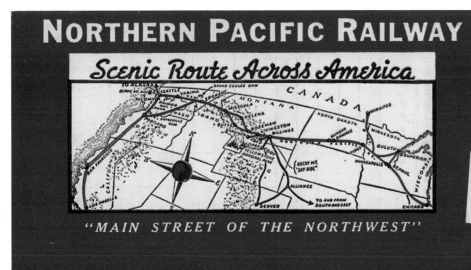

The North Coast Limited *was continually upgraded with streamlining, dome cars, stewardess-nurse service, and modernization of car interiors to keep up with the changing times. One Northern Pacific slogan remained constant over the years—Courteous, Friendly.*

Visit Yellowstone This Summer

World-famous
Old Faithful
Inn

Cost of Tour via Hotels the Lowest in History!

FOR the 1936 season, the cost of the complete 3½-day tour in Yellowstone National Park via hotels is only $41.50—less than ever before!

Plan to visit this greatest and most interesting of the national parks this summer. Go by train on the Northern Pacific, the original Yellowstone Park Line. Through Pullmans on the air-conditioned North Coast Limited serve the famous Gardiner and Cody gateways, the beginning and end of the dramatic park tour.

Send for Booklet

For literature on Yellowstone or vacation trips anywhere West, address E. E. Nelson, Passenger Traffic Manager, Northern Pacific Railway, St. Paul, Minnesota.

Route of the Air-Conditioned, Roller-Bearing

NORTH COAST LIMITED

•Aboard Again—
THE "GREAT BIG" BAKED POTATO

Northern Pacific's famous, delicious "Great Big" Baked Potato is now restored for your delight on dining cars of the NORTH COAST LIMITED.

TRAVEL AND SHIP VIA
NORTHERN PACIFIC RAILWAY—"Main Street of the Northwest"

FORM 6800 PRINTED IN U.S.A.

For years the NP was known as "The Route of the Great Big Baked Potato," the most widely publicized course of the "famously good" dining car meals—a slogan, by the way, that was no exaggeration. These giant spuds weighed an average of two pounds and were almost a meal in themselves at the affordable price of ten cents. Today there are memorabilia collectors who specialize in searching for the many baked potato promotion items—pennants, ink wells, letter openers, blotters, and pencils, to name a few.

Always drumming up passenger traffic, the NP printed numerous brochures for special events, expositions, and conventions.

83

NP's quick service always was featured in the line's promotional literature.

Route of the *faster* NORTH COAST LIMITED

FAST FREIGHT –
Across the West!

USE THROUGH PACKAGE CARS in Northern Pacific fast transcontinental freight trains to assure speedy movement of your shipments.

RAIN OR SHINE, every day in the year, these through cars ply to and from national markets and distributing centers. From New York, Chicago, St. Louis, Kansas City, Denver, St. Paul, Minneapolis, Duluth and Superior they begin their various journeys and in prompt order their contents are delivered to points in Minnesota, North Dakota, Canadian Northwest, Montana, Idaho, Washington, Oregon, California, and British Columbia.

FREE STORE-DOOR PICKUP AND DELIVERY. At Northern Pacific destinations and points of origin our free store-door pickup and delivery of less than carload freight automatically swings into action in a smooth, quick performance

accurately co-ordinated with Northern Pacific train movements. Statewide across Montana this performance is supplemented by the motor truck transportation of the Northern Pacific Transport Company.

50 YEARS' EXPERIENCE. In the exacting job of perishable freight handling alone, the Northern Pacific has had more than half a century of experience! Season after season it has been called upon to enrich the tables of the nation with Northwest fruits, vegetables, sea foods, dairy products and meats, delivered in fresh, prime condition.

THE COMPLETENESS, dependability and long experience of our service means value to you in routing your shipments **Northern Pacific.**

J. G. Morrison
Freight Traffic Manager

R. W. Clark
General Traffic Manager

St. Paul, Minnesota

NORTHERN PACIFIC RAILWAY
First of the Northern Transcontinentals

Northern Pacific Railway
Dining Car Service

Relishes
Head Lettuce with "Our Own" Dressing, 40c; Half Portion, 25c
Queen Olives, 25c   Sweet Mixed Pickles, 15c   Chow Chow, 15c

Soups
(Our Soups Are All Freshly Made—Not Canned)
Hot Chicken Broth, in Cup, 20c   Chicken Broth with Rice, 30c
Consomme, Clear, in Cup, 20c   Tomato Bouillon, in Cup, 20c
Puree of Split Pea, 30c   Clam Chowder, 30c

Fish
Fresh Fish in Season, 70c; Half Portion, 50c   Imported Sardines, 50c

Meats
Mutton Chops (one) 40c; (two) 75c
Milk Fed Chicken (one-half), 90c   Sirloin Steak, $1.00
Fried Calf's Liver and Bacon, 70c   Broiled Pork Chops (2), 75c
Salisbury Steak, Creole Sauce, 65c
Rasher (Two) of Bacon (Served with Meat or Fish Orders Only), 25c

Vegetables
Early June Peas, 20c   Stewed Corn, 20c   String Beans, 25c
Boiled Potatoes, 15c; Mashed Potatoes, 15c
Hashed Brown Potatoes, 20c   Lyonnaise, 20c
French Fried Potatoes, 25c

Salads
Celery and Apple Salad, 35c   Cold Asparagus Vinaigrette, 45c
Potato Salad, 20c

Entremets
Orange Marmalade, 25c   Preserved Figs, 40c (with Cream) 50c
Guava Jelly, 30c

Breads and Pastries
"Our Own" Plum Pudding, Fruit Sauce, 20c
Bread and Butter, 10c   Apple Pie, 20c   Fruit Cake, 20c
Paul's Assorted Fruit Jams, 25c

Cheese
Anona Cheese with Crackers, 25c; Half Portion, 15c
Roquefort Cheese, 30c

Beverages
(Hot Water for Drinking Purposes Furnished Our Guests on Request)
Coffee, Per Pot, 15c   Tea, Per Pot, 15c   Chocolate, 15c
Cocoa, 15c   Instant Postum, 15c   Cream, Per Glass, 35c
Milk Served in Individual Bottle, 15c   Malted Milk, 15c

L. K. OWEN, *Superintendent Dining Cars*, St. Paul, Minnesota

*Mailing envelopes for this genuine photograph
may be had on application to the dining car conductor*

Luxury was promoted on the North Coast Limited, including the food service. Table settings were elaborate with fine china, monogrammed silverware, and linen table cloths displaying the road's trademark.

Yellowstone Park brochure, 1882.

Time schedule, spring-summer 1891.

This brochure touted the line's "2000 miles of startling beauty, featuring twenty-eight mountain ranges and 1,406 miles of rivers," which closely followed "The Trail of Lewis and Clark."

As seen on this cocktail coaster, early F units proudly displayed the famous "christmas tree" paint scheme created by industrial designer Raymond Loewy.

General Motors' Train of Tomorrow at Lakeview, Washington, December 7, 1947.

Scattered among my thousands of railroad pictures are a few that, while not artistic masterpieces, evoke nostalgia and fond memories. Such is the case with this photograph of a General Motors exhibition train passing by the Lakeview Station, which was located in the extreme southern part of Tacoma where the Fort Lewis line branches off from the Tacoma to Tenino Prairie line, not far from present Villa Plaza. I spent many hours in this depot in the summer of 1943 while second trick operator Bob Fristad taught me the telegraph operator trade.

The gentleman in the white shirt is Agent Frank Emerick who was the local chairman for the Order of Railroad Telegraphers and recruited me into that union after I had become an operator. Standing next to him is Chuck Stillman holding his son Don. Chuck was my boss for many years in the Tacoma Union Station dispatchers' office. Next to the switch stand, camera in hand, is Don McGregor, who was to become assistant chief dispatcher. Don's good humor and caring concern for his friends and fellow workers will always be remembered. Don's son, Charles, is standing on the station platform watching this wonder train of the future glide through. My, how the years fly by! Don Stillman went on to become Director of Governmental and International Affairs for the United Auto Workers Union, working with the White House and

foreign governments, and Charles McGregor became a senior engineer for the Boeing Aircraft Company.

The Train of Tomorrow was an experimental demonstrator that went on a six-month tour of the country to show its "mechanical marvels, new-as-tomorrow interior and many postwar features for the comfort and safety of passengers."

Douglass Welch, in his incomparable style, wrote an account of its visit to the Northwest for the *Seattle Post-Intelligencer*. He said, in part:

> General Motors could have put wheels on Lana Turner—a horrid thought—and rolled her from Tacoma to Seattle yesterday and achieved no more Hollywood effect than their celebrated experiment, the Train of Tomorrow, imparts to the astonished visitor.
>
> Four cars and a diesel-electric locomotive, it is a production number throughout, a decorator's dream, unreal and unbelievable even when you're on it, skimming luxuriously through the Kent valley at a 75-mile-an-hour clip. A million Americans have already seen it and millions of dollars have gone into its building and its exhibition in 40 cities, and its run is not over yet. Until August of next year it will continue to demonstrate what imagination can yet do for American railroad business.

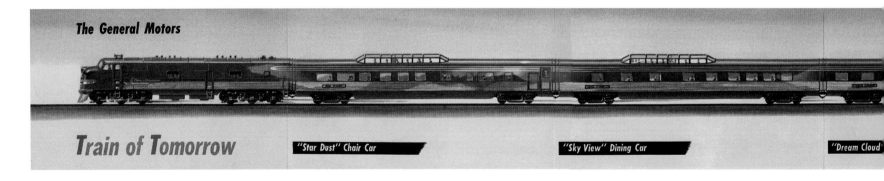

The General Motors

Train of Tomorrow   "Star Dust" Chair Car   "Sky View" Dining Car   "Dream Cloud"

"Moon Glow" Observation Car

"Moon Glow"

For friendly relaxation, there are 2 cocktail lounges furnished much like their counterparts in the smart supper clubs. There is a writing desk in a semi-private nook; telephone service is available to your home or business. The rear observation compartment affords a magnificent view of the swiftly changing landscape, through wide picture windows. Here, as everywhere else on the Train of Tomorrow, nothing has been overlooked that might contribute toward your enjoyment of the trip.

Observation lounge, dedicated to your pleasure en route

NP 26, "North Coast Limited," at Stampede, Washington, April 1962.

Although my personal favorite photos are of steam engines, this picture of the *North Coast Limited* at Stampede from a high angle viewpoint is probably my "best." It appeared on the cover of the *Tacoma News Tribune/Sunday Ledger* on June 3, 1962, and a year later in *Trains* magazine. Then it was used on the cover of a trade magazine called *Textiles Review*, published in North Carolina, whose editor had seen it in *Trains*.

My ego was sent soaring by a letter to the editor of *Trains* by a prominent Wisconsin railfan named Jim Scribbins, who said:

> I'd like to compliment both *Trains* and Photographer J.M. Fredrickson for what I think is one of the very best photos to appear in 23 years of *Trains*. He has managed composition to a highest degree, bringing into his viewfinder enough of the surroundings to readily identify the location and at the same time managing to keep away from the standard 3/4 angle—and still not forgetting that the train is the important item of his photo. Let's have more photos like this and fewer of the oddball 'fancy composition' variety.

Those were kind words by Mr. Scribbins, but the truth of the matter is that in Western Washington, plain old good luck is the key to a successful train picture. If a day isn't mucked up by fog or rain, a good photo location more often than not is spoiled by trees, brush, or a pole line in the way. As a matter of fact, the view from this spot at Stampede now is obscured by trees.

I've made lots of mistakes taking pictures, including some colossal mental blunders, but the occasional success makes it all worthwhile. At least it's sure been fun trying.

All Aboard for Your Northwest Adventure, *February 1959.*

Railroad lore and legends are dominated by tales of high-wheeling throttle artists like Casey Jones and superpower locomotives such as the Yellowstones, Challengers, Northerns, and Big Boys. But wars are won by privates in the trenches and the unglamorous Z-3s were the railroads' counterpart of the "grunts" in the infantry—essential but not much to write about.

They were Mallet compound locomotives with two engines under one boiler, using steam first in the high-pressure small cylinders of the rear engine and the same steam again in the huge low-pressure cylinders of the front engine. This dual use of the steam made them economical to operate, but, with small fifty-seven inch drive wheels designed for climbing steep grades, they were slow and rough riding.

The first Z-3s were built in 1913. They probably would have been phased out or relegated to branch lines when the superpower Z-6 Challengers appeared in the mid-1930s except for one "ace" they held in their deck—they could go through the Stampede Tunnel while the new engines, because of their huge size, could not. This extended their main line service until the coming of the diesels in 1944.

Although not handsome engines, a Z-3 was an impressive sight leaving Easton or Lester with a full-tonnage train headed for Stam-

pede Pass. Three of them were needed to climb the mountain; one on the head end and two on the rear as helpers—one ahead of the caboose and one behind. The rear helper would cut off on the fly just before entering the big tunnel and the helper ahead of the caboose would go through to Stampede on a westbound train or Martin on an eastward train. Then, after cutting out of the train, the fireman on this helper used a squirt hose on the engine to wash the soot from the caboose which had accumulated during the smoky trip through the tunnel.

When this photo was taken, the 4016 had just emerged from a complete overhaul at the South Tacoma Shops, which accounts for its shiny appearance. With daily runs through the two-mile Stampede Tunnel and five smaller tunnels, it wasn't long until they were dull and dingy again. This is probably the reason why the NP name was not painted on the sides of the tenders as on all its other engine classes. The 4016 was built by Alco-Brooks in 1917 and dismantled at South Tacoma on July 11, 1949.

Their slow speed, rough ride, and grimy appearance earned them an uncomplimentary but fitting nickname—the Z-3s were known to all as "sows."

Union Pacific streamliner at Tacoma, April 12, 1942.

On February 12, 1934, the Union Pacific took delivery of its first stream-liner, the *City of Salina,* and the Burlington Route was only two months behind in receiving its first sleek, stainless steel *Zephyr.* These two trains revolutionized passenger service styling, and most other major railroads were quick to join the trend with high-speed trains designed to attract passengers. The Milwaukee Road's *Hiawathas,* Chicago and Northwestern's *400,* Illinois Central's *Panama Limited,* New York Central's *20th Century Limited,* Rock Island's *Rockets,* Santa Fe's *Super Chief,* Seaboard Airline's *Silver Meteor,* and Southern Pacific's *Daylights* were among the pre-World War II glamour trains that succeeded in re-vitalizing the railroad passenger business.

About the only major population center that was not benefiting from dramatically upgraded service was the Seattle-Tacoma area. The north-ern transcontinental lines declined to go along with the majority and Great Northern's *Empire Builder,* Northern Pacific's *North Coast Lim-ited,* and Milwaukee's *Olympian* continued on their same old sched-ules with the same heavyweight cars. This equipment was reasonably comfortable and the food in the dining cars was unexcelled, but they just weren't in tune with the times. Editorials in Seattle and Tacoma newspapers lambasted these roads for their backward attitudes, but to no avail. The railroads' response was that they had a gentlemen's agreement not to outdo one another regarding passenger service. One thing in particular, however, made the pill especially difficult for Seattle and Tacoma to swallow—Portland was being served by one of the best of the new streamliners, the Union Pacific's *City of Portland.*

Finally, Union Pacific made the first break-through for Puget Sound streamliner service. On April 12, 1942, a Seattle-Portland connection was established for the *City of Portland* using one of the older sets of equipment shown here on its first trip through Tacoma.

An article in the April 8, 1942, *Tacoma Times* said in part:

> Every sixth day, beginning next Sunday, a streamlined passenger train will whiz back and forth between Portland and Seattle with only one stop each way—that at Tacoma . . . Roughly once a week there will be an opportunity to ride a streamliner and get the feel of it; to become acquainted with the new age in railroad passenger equipment.

The new age finally came to the northern lines shortly after World War II as the GN, NP, and Milwaukee equipped their premier trains with streamlined equipment on accelerated schedules. This, combined with the traditional good food and service, gave the Northwest unsur-passed passenger service.

Milwaukee Road E-2, Bi-Polar Electric, at Tacoma, June 1, 1943.

"Possessor of so many records that it has practically upset the accepted traditions and theories of railroad building and established itself as one of the 'Seven Wonders' of the 20th century, the Chicago, Milwaukee and Puget Sound Railway is finishing the last lap of what veteran railroad men claim to be the most wonderful race across a continent to tidewater the world has ever seen." These glowing words appeared in the 1909 Commercial Club special edition of the *Tacoma Ledger*. The author no doubt would have thought it insane if anyone would have predicted that this railroad colossus would crumble in a short seventy years.

The Milwaukee was an old-time road in the Midwest that early in the Twentieth Century decided to build a west-coast extension. This last of the transcontinental routes was an extremely costly project as the goal was a line that would be shorter and faster than those of its competitors, the Great Northern and Northern Pacific. The Milwaukee hoped to gain an edge in the competition for the high priority special trains that carried Oriental silk from Puget Sound ports to the east. Furthermore, it was built without government land grants, and the installation of electric locomotive operations between Harlowton, Montana, and Avery, Idaho, and between Othello, Washington, and Tacoma added to the cost. These financial burdens were never overcome, and the Pacific Extension was finally abandoned in 1980.

There is no disputing the fact that the Milwaukee had distinctive, innovative features and the road wasn't bashful about letting the public know about them. In 1926 newspaper ads promoting its premier passenger train, the *Olympian,* the Milwaukee proclaimed:

- The only line operating transcontinental trains by electric power.
- The only line owning and operating its own sleeping cars from Seattle and Tacoma to Chicago.
- The only line operating over its own rails all the way between Puget Sound and Chicago.
- The shortest line from Seattle and Tacoma to Chicago.
- The *Olympian* is drawn across the mountain ranges by electric power—behind the mightiest locomotives in the world—smokeless, sootless, cinderless. Its course is without jar or jolt, smooth, swift, dependable.

The pride of its locomotive fleet were the Bi-Polars (a name derived from their electrical design) built by General Electric in 1917–18 and almost instantly a public relations triumph. For a time, not only were they "the mightiest electric locomotives in the world" as the above ad boasted, but they had a distinctive design that caught the public's eye. The Milwaukee staged steam-versus-electric shoving contests and, of course, the Bi-Polars always won.

Noel Holley of Seattle has published an excellent book, titled *The Milwaukee Electrics: An Inside Look at Locomotives and Railroading.* Albert Farrow and I, as well as Warren McGee and Ron Nixon, contributed photos to the book. Albert's Bi-Polar shots are particularly outstanding.

Not to be outdone by the Milwaukee Road's attractions, a Northern Pacific advertisement in the *Seattle Post-Intelligencer*, March 26, 1928, advised the traveling public to:

> Plan your eastward journey for comfort and luxury on the *North Coast Limited*, see 28 mountain ranges—follow 1,406 miles of historic and scenic rivers—through cool evergreen forests.
>
> "Famously Good" meals on this all-steel train and personal service you'll appreciate—maid, barber, valet services, library, baths, card rooms, soda-fountain, buffet and luxurious observation-club car furnished like the finest hotel. Extra Comforts—No Extra Fare.

For years the NP was known as "The Route of the Great Big Baked Potato," the most widely publicized course of the "famously good" dining car meals—a slogan, by the way, that was no exaggeration. These giant spuds weighed an average of two pounds and were almost a meal in themselves at the affordable price of ten cents. Today there are memorabilia collectors who specialize in searching for the many baked potato promotion items—pennants, ink wells, letter openers, blotters, and pencils, to name a few.

The *North Coast Limited* was continually upgraded over the years with streamlining, dome cars, stewardess-nurse service, and modernization of car interiors to keep up with the changing times. One Northern Pacific slogan remained constant over the years—Courteous, Friendly. Charlie Hough, John Schwartz, Kenny Goodson, Mar Hebert, Bill Jaeger, Roy O'Grady, Pat Cloherty, Harold Nordgren, and Jim Taylor, to name just a few veteran passenger trainmen, made these words a reality. (One of the more unusual events in NP passenger train history took place at Seattle in 1958 when Conductor Jim Taylor married Stewardess-Nurse Lorain Nygaard in the observation-lounge car of the *North Coast Limited* at King Street Station.)

Charlie Hough himself was the subject of an NP promotional story for being the youngest passenger service conductor on the railroad in 1956. Charlie's railroad roots run deep. His father, W.G. Hough, went to work for the NP in 1907 and was a brakeman on the Arlington Local when Charlie was born in Auburn in 1920, the beginning of a remarkable life story. He became a talented baseball player during his high school years and was given a tryout with the Cincinnati Reds at the same time as the legendary major leaguer, Fred Hutchinson. Charlie was forced to drop out of a trip to an eastern baseball camp because of an illness that resulted in an eighteen pound weight loss. In 1940 he hired out as a brakeman on the NP shortly after he and Dean Shannon had joined the Naval Reserves. He worked only seven days as a brakeman before the Navy called him to active service, which led to two tours of duty during World War II. Charlie saw war action from ringside in twelve out of twenty-one major conflicts in the Pacific including the long Guadalcanal campaign—he was assigned to one of the landing craft that put the marines ashore under fierce enemy gunfire.

After the war he returned to the railroad and spent the next fifteen years as passenger brakeman and conductor. During this time he became deeply involved in working for the Brotherhood of Railroad Trainmen and was called on in 1967 by union president Park Kennedy to organize the legislative arm of what later became the United Transportation Union. In 1969 he left active railroad service to become a state legislative director for the union, a position he held until retiring in 1982. Charlie, however, really didn't retire. He became president of the Auburn Chapter of the Burlington Northern Veterans, and because of continuing concern for the welfare of his fellow "rails" was an eloquent spokesman for the National Association of Retired Veteran Railroad Employees (NARVRE). He kept up the good work!

NP observation-lounge car, Tacoma Club, at Missoula, Montana, August 20, 1948.

When I first went to work for the Northern Pacific, veteran "rails" would tell me: "Stick with the railroad, kid, you will always have free medical care and you can get a free pass to go by train to anyplace in the United States, Canada, and Mexico."

Well, the old NP hospital is long gone, and in 1971 the railroads unloaded their extensive passenger service—to be replaced by the limited service AMTRAK provides. To add insult to injury, the old policy of free exchange passes on all railroads was replaced by AMTRAK's "free on home road only" policy, with half-fare on connecting roads. The half-rates were calculated on the highest fare AMTRAK had, so in many cases it was better to pay the cut-rate All Aboard America fare and get out from under the other burdensome restriction of "no reservations for pass passengers until 24 hours before train time." So, those early day promises about free passes and medical care were almost as wrong as a prediction an old-time operator once told me: "The NP will never get any of them diesels."

I don't mean to sound critical of AMTRAK, as I think they did a remarkable job considering the condition of the equipment they inherited and the lack of enthusiastic governmental support. It's just that so much tradition and glamour were lost when the railroads themselves ceased to be passenger train operators. In the pre-AMTRAK days, each major railway company had at least one premier train that was considered its "showcase" to give the public a good impression of the entire road. These trains were equipped with the best cars available, elegant diners, and luxury observation-lounge cars at the rear. In pre-streamliner days, the observation cars usually had an open platform with chairs and a searchlight for viewing the passing scenery at night.

Riding in the open on a steam train was usually a somewhat dusty and grimy experience, not to mention the wind caused by a train's high speed. The Milwaukee, however, had full-length open-air observation cars in its electrified territory through the mountains and emphasized in its advertising how much cleaner its electric trains were than the steam-powered competitors. The Lackawanna Road used a cleanliness gimmick in passenger train promotions centered around the line's use of hard, cinderless anthracite coal in its steam engines. The symbol of their service was a fictitious, white-clad passenger named Phoebe Snow; the ads contained verses such as "Miss Snow alights, her dress still white, she rode the road of anthracite." The open-air platforms disappeared with the coming of streamlining and the use of enclosed, round-ended observation cars.

Another tradition that has faded into nostalgia is the naming of Pullman sleeping cars. NP named its post-war observation cars after prestigious social clubs located in cities in its territory. Besides the Tacoma Club, there were the Rainier Club, Arlington Club, Spokane Club, Minneapolis Club, and the Montana Club. The sleeping cars were named after cities on the line—Aberdeen, Billings, Jamestown, and Pasco, to name a few. The Great Northern leaned toward geographical features for names, such as Gunsight Pass, Agassiz Glacier, Grand Coulee, Skagit River, and Big Horn Pass. My personal favorites were the pre-war NP sleepers in the "Chief" series, among which were Chief Rocky Bear, Chief Standing Buffalo, and Chief Little Raven. Other Pullmans in service on the NP had names that just sounded nice, like Poplar Hollow and Clover Glen.

Pacific Coast Railroad train at a Renton, Washington, water tank in 1949.

When Northern Pacific selected Tacoma as its Western terminus it was a stunning blow to Seattle. Some merchants even closed their doors and moved to Tacoma, convinced that Seattle would never be anything more than a sawmill town. A number of leading citizens, however, wouldn't give up without a fight—among them Arthur A. Denny and Dexter Horton—and they decided that if a railroad would not come to them, they would build one of their own.

At the time, thriving Walla Walla was one of the largest communities in Washington Territory. A plan was formulated to build a line connecting Walla Walla with Seattle by way of Snoqualmie Pass and thus bring Inland Empire grain and other products to the coast at lower rates than what the Northern Pacific charged. The South Walla Walla Railroad and Transportation Company was organized and work on it started on May 1, 1874, with the entire Seattle community turning out to clear and level a roadbed, beginning on the Duwamish River not far from present-day Georgetown. The road never realized its dream of crossing Snoqualmie Pass, but it did open a prosperous trade with the coal mines at Renton, Newcastle, and later Black Diamond. In 1880 the name of the road was changed from the Seattle and Walla Walla Railroad to the Columbia and Puget Sound, and in 1916 it was renamed the Pacific Coast Railroad. In later years, all of its stock was acquired by the Great Northern and consequently it eventually became part of the Burlington Northern system.

Another Washington railroad line missed out on being part of the Burlington Northern because the NP sold it to the International Paper Company prior to the merger. The former Yacolt Branch of the NP in the southwest part of the state, like the Pacific Coast, was conceived as a short line. The Vancouver, Klickitat and Yakima; the Portland, Vancouver and Yakima; and the Washington and Oregon Railroad and Navigation Company were its earlier names before its acquisition by the Northern Pacific. It was purchased by the paper company in the 1950s to serve a mill at Chelatchie Prairie, northeast of Vancouver, but it was no longer needed when the mill later closed. Its line from Rye on the outskirts of Vancouver to Chelatchie Prairie was finally purchased by Clark County and operated as the Lewis and Clark Railway with Ed Berntsen as its president. Its railfan excursion passenger trains became immensely popular with two trains a day making round trips from the Battle Ground passenger station to Moulton Falls County Park, passing over three trestles, through a rock tunnel, and along the Lewis River valley.

NP train Number 3 at Martin, Washington, February 15, 1945.

Early in 1945, section foreman Vito Ferri, section men Narcisso "Scotty" Giometti and Amobilio Innocenti (and his wife Mrs. "Mobile"), and telegraphers Charles McGurk, Barney Roland, and yours truly were the entire population of the community of Martin at the east portal of the Stampede Tunnel. I went to work there after graduating from high school at the mid-term. It was an unforgettable experience.

The living conditions were incredibly crude—especially in the winter—with no electricity and our major plumbing facility located out-of-doors. The first item of business after arising from bed was, more often than not, shoveling a path through a foot or two of new snow to reach the outhouse. The living quarters were heated by large, antiquated coal stoves. It was the usual practice to dump two buckets of coal in a stove at bedtime, hoping there would still be some live coals when it was time to get up. The trouble with this procedure was being awakened a few hours later by a loud "whoomp" from the coal gasses exploding.

Another huge "minus" to living here in the winter was the deep snow covering the access roads. This, along with no days off (telegraphers were working a seven-day week at this time), would have meant virtual hibernation if it hadn't been for traveling by train. The second trick shift had the only sure schedule for getting out, as it was possible to go to Easton, Cle Elum, or Ellensburg on the morning Train Number 4 and return on Number 5 in time for work. The day shift had to depend on light helper engines to get out to Easton or Lester. My first shift was third trick (midnight to 8:00 a.m.) and my nightly hope was that Number 3 would be more than four hours late and reach Martin after I was off duty, so I could get aboard. I well remember listening impatiently on the phone at midnight, waiting for the Yakima depot operator to give the dispatcher the ETAs on the westbound passenger trains—from this information I could determine if I could go to Tacoma on Number 3, and then return on the evening Train Number 6. Actually, Number 3 often was late, as the wartime overload made on-time performance a rarity.

On the day I took this photo, I had elected to stay in Martin and watched Number 3 go by from the doorway of my living quarters. There was one "plus" to life at Martin in the winter—the surroundings had a Christmas-card like beauty, especially after a fresh, new snowfall, as this picture shows. Unfortunately, the timing of my stay at Martin was wrong. I would have much more appreciated living in the wilderness at a later stage of life, instead of when I was a teenager.

Rotary snowplow at Stampede, January 19, 1972.

Weather conditions were so severe in the Cascade Range in February 1949 that the *Seattle Times* sent a reporter to Stampede Pass to get an on-the-scene account. Robert Barr's dramatic story, headlined "Stampede Sees Railroading at Its Roughest," said in part:

> High in a frozen wilderness of howling winds and bleak mountain peaks, all but suffocated under what men say is the worst snowfall and bitterest winter in the history of Stampede, is railroading at its meanest and toughest . . . Few can remember anything worse. Last night there were 159 inches of snow—more than 13 feet—at Stampede, the west portal of the Stampede tunnel. The deepest the weather bureau could find for February was 96 inches in 1933. There are 196 inches—16 feet, 4 inches—at Martin, the east portal. Vito Ferri, veteran section Foreman, said he had slept about four hours the past week . . . Gus Kavadias, a tired, snow-weary roadmaster is proud of the work they are doing against such odds . . . A spreader plow comes through the east portal to work eight miles of double track to Easton. It'll pass a west bound rotary plow. You climb on the spreader and watch Howard Barkey, who can peel a dollar bill off a signal standard with one of the two big blades without hitting the standard . . . At Easton, Mark Hare the trainmaster and boss of the track clearing operation talks orders slowly into a telephone. Railroad men, in the popular version, usually bark orders. He's too tired to bark. Everybody is.

Everything about railroading has been constantly changing, even the weather. Because of mostly mild winters in recent decades, rotary plows rarely have been needed to keep the line open. In early 1972, however, Trainmaster Jerry Bergman and Roadmaster Bob Robey battled to keep Stampede Pass open for trains. Fortunately, I was able to ride along on the rotary plow with my camera and take pictures of what has become a rare event. Since then, spreaders and an on-track machine similar to a ballast regulator normally have been adequate to do the job.

NP 5138 on wye at Easton, April 15, 1944.

In reflecting back over the many years since I began railroading, I would have to say that my favorite place on the Northern Pacific, next to the Tacoma Union Station, was Easton. There was so much activity there 24 hours a day in the pre-diesel times. What a sight it was watching Number 5 roaring into town with Red Bevan at the throttle. I wondered how in the world he could stop in time, but, in an instant, the tender would be spotted perfectly under the water tank.

Then there was Conductor "Sambo" Sampson swinging his gangly legs gracefully onto the caboose between two struggling Z-3 helpers with their sixteen drivers clanking, as the train gained speed by the depot. And for the second trick operator, there was the breathtaking thrill of hooping up train orders to double-header engines on the *North Coast Limited*, throwing a mail sack through the open door of the mail car, and then hooping up to the brakeman as the "pride of the Northern Pacific" picked up speed coming off the mountain.

The frosting on the cake for a young engine-picture-taking telegrapher was being paid to be at a place where the Z-8 Challenger engines, barely a year old, were cut off westbound freights because they were too big for the Stampede Tunnel and replaced by smaller Z-3s for the trip over the hill. These magnificent machines were turned on the wye, serviced at the coal dock, and then waited for their eastbound assignments. My photo of the 5138 on the wye is one of my all-time favorites and it was used by *Trains* magazine in a double-page spread in April 1965.

In the years since taking this picture, I have become quite chagrined for having failed to jot down the names of the people in the photographs. I showed this picture to various "old heads" hoping for identification, but to no avail, until finally NP/BN Engineer Melvin Ashley immediately recognized his cousin Warren Graybeal standing by the front of the engine. This revelation brought back instant memories as the Graybeal family operated a grocery store in Easton, and, after World War II, Warren married my fellow telegrapher Velta Mae Sparkman. He and "Sparky" left the railroad for the trucking business and later retired in Shawnee, Oklahoma. I sent them a copy of the photo and received a most interesting letter reminiscing about the glory-days of Easton. Oh, yes, they remembered the "kid with the camera."

Now, whenever we zip by Easton on Interstate 90 driving at 70 mph, a feeling of sadness prevails and I can't help wondering why such a good place had to die.

Spokane, Portland and Seattle 905,
Class Z-6, at Parkwater (Spokane, Washington),
May 27, 1953.

Articulated locomotives like SP&S 905 were actually two engines under one boiler. It was a spectacular sight to watch the two sets of drivers working in unison on a steep grade. One of my earliest train-riding recollections was aboard the *North Coast Limited* over the "Butte Mountain," peering ahead out the window to watch an NP 5100 (twin of SP&S 905) leaning around the sharp curves with its twelve mighty drivers conquering the Rocky Mountains.

NP 2667, Class A-3, at Missoula, Montana, August 20, 1949.

In a "turn back the calendar" interview with retired Trainmaster Ed Overlie, the subject came around to NP's incomparable 2600-series "Northern" (named for the NP) type locomotives. Ed had his most memorable engine ride when he was roadmaster in charge of the territory between Spokane, Washington, and Sandpoint, Idaho. It was his regular routine to ride the rear car of Number 2 from Spokane to Sandpoint once a week and return home on the engine of Number 1 (*North Coast Limited*) to check on how smoothly the trains were riding over his track. Number 1 with the 2667 was running behind schedule on this particular day, and as soon as they passed Rathdrum, Idaho, with only slight curves the rest of the way, the engineer pulled the throttle back about as far as it would go. The speedometers in those days only registered up to 85 mph and before long the needle was against the peg.

Ed asked the engineer how fast he estimated they were going. He replied, "I just timed the last mile with my watch and we are right on 100 mph."

I asked Ed if he was a little nervous going that fast. In his laid-back manner he said, "Oh no, with an A-3 engine on my good track there was nothing to worry about."

Most of my train dispatching career was on the Yakima to Auburn "Mountain" district on third trick, and I never ceased getting a thrill out of watching a skilled "throttle artist" make up time on the *North Coast Limited* when it was running late. One of my favorites was my good friend Ed Foisie. A good engineer would run from Yakima to East Auburn in 3 hours and 10 minutes, but Ed could do it in 2 hours, 59 minutes.

Another good friend, Bill Dahlberg, was the unchallenged best of them all when it came to a combination of maintaining high speed with smooth handling. I was riding with him one night on Number 2. When we arrived at Yakima, the conductor came up and said to him, "I never thought we could come down the canyon that fast and that smooth."

Whenever there was a highly important special train (e.g., the President of the United States, the NP Board of Directors, etc.), Bill would be taken off his regular run to take charge of it. Probably his most notable duty was handling Franklin D. Roosevelt's train during the president's super-secret trip to the Northwest to inspect the war effort in 1942, although I since have wondered how much Bill appreciated that assignment. I climbed up on his engine one night in 1944 wearing an FDR campaign button. He scowled and said, "What are you wearing that thing for?" President Roosevelt was famous for being either loved or hated, with no middle ground, and I guess Bill and I represented the opposite poles.

At least it didn't spoil our friendship.

The name of the game is change. Virtually nothing is the same as it was when I began with the NP in 1943, and that includes the work horse of the railroad, the freight train. Today there is an endless procession of container, piggyback, coal, and grain trains. Yesterday, when Tacoma was the "Lumber capital of America," it was forest products—lumber, shingles, plywood, and doors—that made up the typical eastbound freight drag. And, of course, they all started as logs which also moved by rail.

Log trains were the train dispatcher's nightmare on double track—to avoid a wreck from a log falling off one of the flimsy flat cars, log trains were required to stand still while opposing trains passed. It took an involved web of train orders on the "double track south" to thread the countless NP, Milwaukee, and LP&N "loggers" through this high-volume territory. Log trains ran everywhere in western Washington. Retired engineer Charlie Everest in the NP Historical Association's journal, *The Mainstreeter*, tells of pulling one-hundred car log trains from Lake Kapowsin to Tacoma day after day with little F-1 "hog" engines.

Logging camps were especially frequent on the old NP First Subdivision (Auburn to Yakima). Eagle Gorge with its two camps, and Nagrom, Maywood, Lester, Cabin Creek, and Swauk, as well as Kanaskat accumulating cars from Selleck on the Green River Branch, produced a seemingly endless parade of loaded log flats outbound and empties inbound. At one time there was an Auburn-Lester Turn, a Lester Switcher, and a Cle Elum-Lester Turn, in addition to Auburn-Cle Elum and Yakima-Cle Elum locals, all handling logs.

Many of the larger camps had their own railroads climbing high into the woods to bring logs down to the main line. The steep grades required slow but sturdy geared locomotives. There was enough of a demand for logging locomotives to keep four manufacturers in business—Lima Shay, Climax, Heisler, and Willamette.

A discussion on logging engines would not be complete without mentioning former NP/BN engineer Albert Farrow of Auburn. Albert, following in his father's footsteps, went to work at the Auburn Roundhouse in 1935 and quickly learned all about steam engines—as he was a fire-builder, engine watchman, and a helper to machinists, boilermakers, and pipefitters. In 1936 he went out on the road as fireman, and in 1943 was promoted to the right side of the cab as engineer. Al took up locomotive photography at an early age and soon zeroed in on logging engines as his specialty. A unique photographic talent, combined with a dogged determination to seek out the elusive log train in its remote environment, produced a collection second to none. Any worthwhile book on logging railroads will have captions reading "photo by Albert Farrow." Al taught me photographic fundamentals for which I am eternally grateful. I only wish I could have met him sooner—my earlier pictures would have been much better.

NP train Number 4, "Alaskan," at East Auburn, June 20, 1946.

In the pre-AMTRAK days when each railroad had its own fleet of passenger trains, their publicity efforts always featured the "showcase" or "limited" trains that made few stops and had first-rate furnishings. But providing most of the service to the most towns were the "locals," and NP's Number 4 (Seattle to Saint Paul) was a classic example. (Passengers from Tacoma were taken to East Auburn on a "stub" connection—visible behind Number 4 in the picture—and there were enough people changing trains to support a refreshment stand at the station).

Number 4's equipment, except for a reserved-seat coach, was not exactly the pride of the Northern Pacific. The non air conditioned coaches had straight-back green or red plush seats designed to resist wear rather than provide comfort. Ventilation was provided by small hinged vents near the ceiling, which the brakeman opened or closed using a stick with a brass hook on the end. If he forgot to close them before entering a long tunnel, the car filled with smoke! Meals were served in a cafe-coach—half coach and half diner—and the NP's slogan, "famously good food," was strictly upheld, even on this lowly local.

Comfort was available on Number 4 for those willing to pay a 50-cent surcharge to ride in the reserved seat coach. NP published a small brochure for these cars, calling them an "oasis of comfort for travel between Seattle and Spokane, with lounge chairs, carpet, streamline interiors and well-equipped dressing rooms, plus air-conditioning, make these coaches even more luxurious than the handsome parlor cars of a few years ago!" The brochure also mentioned that club breakfast in the cafe-coach "cost only 50 cents; regular plate meals only 65 cents; table d'hôte luncheon only 90 cents and table d'hôte dinner only $1.00."

On the head end of the train was the RPO (Railway Post Office) car with a mail-service clerk aboard to sort mail and handle letters dropped through a slot on the side of the car.

The cars are only a part of the story of Number 4 and similar locals; the varied assortment of passengers, the stations where they boarded, and the scenery en route would be enough material for a book. It seemed as if Number 4 would barely get going before it was time for the next stop—Ravensdale, Kanaskat, Eagle Gorge, Baldi, Humphrey, Sweeney's Ranch, Old Maywood, Maywood, East Maywood, Nagrom, and Hot Springs were all stops for Number 4 in the forty miles between East Auburn and Lester. Multiply this by all of the small communities for the remaining 1,900 miles to Saint Paul and it can easily be seen that Number 4 was not the train for a passenger in a hurry. But for fishermen and loggers in the summer, and skiers in the winter, it was the only way to go.

Wines and Liquors

Cocktails

Manhattan	. . .	.35	Side Car	.35
Martini	. . . .	.30	Old Fashioned .	.35

Liquors and Cordials

Individual Bottle

Bourbon Whiskey (American Bond)	. . .	.40
Bourbon Whiskey (Over 1 year old)	. . .	.30
Blended Whiskey	. . . .	.30
Scotch Whiskey	. . . .	.50
Irish Whiskey (Over 10 years old)	. . . .	.45
Rye Whiskey	. . . .	.40
Canadian Club Whiskey	. . . . . .	.40
Puerto Rico Rum	. . . . . .	.40
Gin	. . . .	.30
Sloe Gin	. . . . . .	.30
Brandy	. . . . . .	.40
Champagne Cognac (50 years old)	. . . .	.50
D. O. M. Benedictine	. . . . . .	.50

Miscellaneous

Gin Fizz	. . .	.40	Golden Fizz	.45
Silver Fizz	. .	.45	Tom Collins	.40
		Sloe Gin Rickey 40		

California Wines

Sauterne	. . . .	Splits .45	Half Bottle .75
Old Claret	. . . .	Splits .45	Half Bottle .75
Burgundy	. . . .	Splits .45	Half Bottle .75

Imported Wines

Amontillado Sherry	. .	Individual Bottle .40
Old Port	. . . .	Individual Bottle .40
ASSORTED BRANDS BOTTLED BEER		.25
Domestic Ale	. . . .	Bottle .30

Mineral Waters and Gingerale

White Rock Water	. . .	Pint .25	Split	.15
Rock Springs Water	. . .	Pint .20	Split	.10
Canada Dry Water	. . .	Pint .20	Split	.10
Club Soda	. . . . . .	Pint .25	Split	.15
Gingerale	. . . . . .	Pint .25	Split	.15
Coca Cola	. . . .		Bottle	.10
Root Beer	. . . .		Bottle	.10
Bromo Seltzer	. . . .		Bottle	.20

Sale of Beer, Wines and Liquors subject to State and Federal Regulations

Northern Pacific Ry.
DINING CAR SERVICE

Form 6509—Revised 10M 1-39

January 1939.

NP Sedro Woolley-Auburn local at Woodinville, Washington, May 1953.

This photo has not one, but three stories to tell. The first is Bill Brandenburg, the agent at Woodinville, who is watching the Sedro Woolley-Auburn local leave town. Bill's roots go far back into railroad history when Morse telegraph was the king of communication. Bill's father, Daniel, was a telegraph operator for the Rock Island Railroad in Iowa and first became acquainted with Bill's mother, Grace, over the Morse wire, as she was a telegrapher for Western Union in its immense Chicago office. (She had to be a "crackerjack" operator to hold a position in that busy place.) After their marriage, Daniel and Grace Brandenburg moved on to the Great Northern; Bill was born in 1918 when his parents were working at Noyes, Minnesota, on the Manitoba border.

By the time Bill was three, his parents had tired of the bitter winter weather and decided to go west, ending up in the NP's relay office at Centralia, Washington, in the days when that town was a pivotal railroad center. When Bill was ready to look for work out of high school, Grace was agent at Moclips and Daniel served as afternoon operator in Hoquiam, where he taught his son the art of telegraphy. Bill's first day as an operator was at the busy McCarver Street Station in Tacoma. For the first few years he "bucked" the extra board, working all over the Tacoma Division—Cle Elum, Wymer, Martin, Thrall, Selah, Yakima, Arlington, Everett, to name a few of the stations. He was later agent at Bothell, Sedro Woolley, Kirkland, Woodinville, and Kent, where he was promoted to exempt agent in 1967. He later became agent at Tacoma in 1975 and retired from this position on August 31, 1979.

The second story is Class C-1 steam locomotive 684 being towed by the Woolley Local to the 684's next exhibition site. The NP at one time owned more than three-hundred 4-4-0 American Standard locomotives. The 684, built in 1883 by the New York Locomotive Works, is the only survivor of this class of engine that literally built the railroad. It had been sold in 1928 to the Nez Perce and Idaho Railroad. After outliving its usefulness on this small line, it was left abandoned off the end of a spur at Nez Perce, Idaho. Fortunately, its existence was known to photographer/historian Ronald Nixon. Largely through his efforts, it was reacquired by the Northern Pacific and restored to "like new" condition as a traveling museum piece.

Ron Nixon is the third story. He, too, was a Morse telegraph operator of exceptional talent—good enough to work for Western Union and the Associated Press, which demanded the utmost in speed and accuracy. Most of his career was spent with the NP both as a relay division operator and, for a while, dispatching in the Missoula office during World War II, when the Rocky Mountain Division was an absolute nightmare of high-priority military traffic. I never knew a more skilled railroader, but, of course, Ron's legacy is the incomparable photographic collection he has left to help future generations know that there once was a great railroad called the Northern Pacific.

Rayonier Logging Co. 90 near Hoquiam, March 31, 1962.

It's always a pleasure to have a photograph published and this was especially true of one appearing on the cover of the *Tacoma News Tribune* magazine section in 1962. I particularly appreciate the caption which read:

With her stack huffing smoke, her whistle blowing and steam popping off from her safety valve, old No. 90 rumbles across a trestle with a load of logs on the Rayonier logging road north of Hoquiam. The photograph by J.M. Fredrickson marks the end of an era. A few minutes after No. 90 crossed the trestle she was uncoupled from the train of logs and a diesel locomotive backed in to take her place. Rayonier had changed its logging operation from steam to diesel. No. 90 was first steamed up in 1926 and did her job faithfully for 36 years.

The ceremony marking the change was held last March 31 and was attended by hundreds of railroad buffs, among whom photographer Fredrickson is one of the most enthusiastic.

Seattle Post-Intelligencer reporter Charles Dunsire also was on hand for the "Last Run" festivities and part of his colorful account read:

Angry at her forced retirement, old Number 90 snorted a column of black, acrid smoke and shrilly hooted her contempt for her sleek successor as she highballed it down the track. More than 2,000 persons, hundreds loaded with still and motion picture cameras, crowded Rayonier's right-of-way along highway 101 north of Hoquiam to witness and record the end of a railroad era . . . As old Number 90 made for the siding, she huffed a last gasp of smoke and her bell clanged in mournful farewell, sounding a death knell for herself and for a railroad era in Western Washington.

Simpson Logging Co. 3 at Shelton, Washington, 1946.

Before the advent of the logging truck, there were literally dozens of logging railroads in the State of Washington. By 1990, there were but three: the Chehalis Western, operating over the old Tacoma Eastern Branch of the Milwaukee; Weyerhaeuser's Columbia and Cowlitz based in Longview; and the Simpson Logging Company Line out of Shelton.

The history of the Simpson operation is a rather tangled web. It was organized in 1895 and operated for many years as a common carrier known as the Peninsular Railway, but some of its segments had even earlier beginnings. The Satsop Railroad was started in 1884 (three years before the NP crossed the Cascades) and by 1886 operated ten miles of logging road in the Shelton area. Bankruptcy in 1889 resulted in its reorganization in 1891 as the Washington Southern Railway. This road had grown to twenty miles in length by 1895 when it was sold at foreclosure to the Peninsular Railway.

The Puget Sound and Gray's Harbor Railroad and Transportation Company was formed in 1887 and operated a fourteen mile logging road in Mason County, terminating at Kamilche. Financial problems seem to be the common denominator of these small lines, as the PS&GH was reorganized into the Blakely Railroad in 1896. This road grew to a length of thirty miles from Kamilche to Matlock by the time it was absorbed by the Peninsular Railway in 1896.

The Mason County Central was a six-and-half mile logging railroad built in 1887-88 and running out of Shelton, but once again reorganization in 1891 brought a name change—the Shelton Southwestern Railroad. After expanding to twelve miles, another financial shuffle took place in 1898, producing the name Shelton South Western Washington Railway. This turned out to be a short-lived company as opera-

tion ceased in 1903. Part of the road was abandoned in 1905 and the remainder became part of the Peninsular Railway.

And finally, the Shamrock and Western was built by McCleary Lumber and absorbed by the Peninsular Railway in the 1930s.

A photo-history of the Peninsular Railway, *Logging to the Saltchuck*, has been completed by Simpson locomotive engineer Pete Replinger and logging road expert John Labbe. No essay about logging roads would be complete without mentioning Al Farrow of Auburn who had the vision and foresight to search out and photograph logging trains during their heyday. Al's collection includes outstanding movies of a 1939 NP passenger train excursion from Tacoma to Shelton, and then onto the Peninsular Railway.

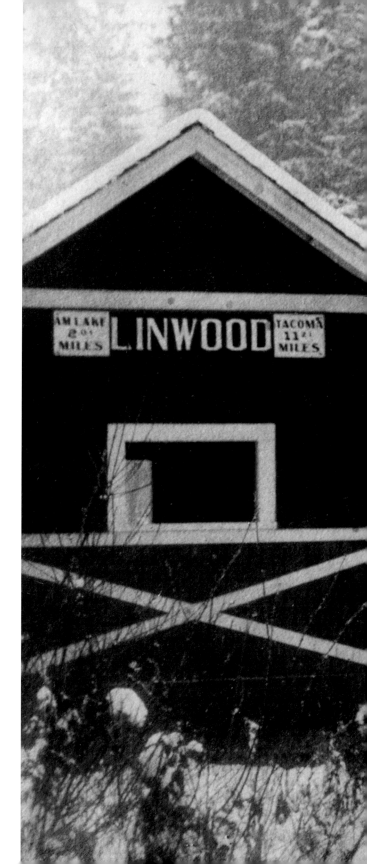

American Lake Line street car at Linwood, Washington, 1908.

Going downtown during my childhood years meant boarding the stubby little "K Street" car at North 10th and K, and then transferring to the cable car at South 13th and K. I well remember the ride down 13th Street hill, as I always rode on the bench-like seat at the center of the cable car to watch the gripman tug on the brake lever. It also was possible to peer down through the mechanism and see the street passing by underneath.

And, of course, downtown Tacoma in those days was an exciting place for children of all ages during the Christmas season. Broadway, between 9th and 13th, was crowded with shoppers loading up on gifts at the many stores. Two large department stores at 11th and Broadway—Rhodes Brothers and Fishers (later Bon Marche)—were the center of shopping activity, highlighted by large front-window toy displays, complete with Santa Claus and electric trains. J.C. Penney and the three "Five and Dime" stores—Kress, Metropolitan, and Woolworth—were equally busy.

For many years, Tacoma was crisscrossed with street car lines—Pt. Defiance, Sixth Avenue, South Tacoma, Fern Hill, Spanaway, McKinley Avenue, Portland Avenue, to name some of them. The photo of an American Lake car at Linwood was given to me by the widow of NP Brakeman Stephen Van Volkenburgh. Van (on the left) worked for the Tacoma Railway and Power Company before hiring out on the NP. "Linwood-on-the-Lake" was located at the southeast corner of Gravelly Lake, where Gravelly Lake Drive intersects Nyanza Road.

The street car era in Tacoma came to a sad and sudden end on June 11, 1938, during a civic celebration for the last run and the changeover to buses. The *Tacoma News Tribune* proclaimed: "What will happen when the last street car goes clanking down the steel ruts here Saturday night, to be replaced Sunday by airflow buses with seats more comfortable than the divans Cleopatra lounged upon the day she bewitched M. Anthony? It will be the City's happiest Moment."

I say—Balderdash!

Train Number 311 (Spokane-Lewiston) at Oakesdale, Washington, June 12, 1955.

During the 1920s and 1930s, a common sight on branch lines was the "galloping goose" or "doodlebug." These were self-propelled, gas-electric, single units usually painted red and white on the front with Pullman green sides. They were uncomfortable and underpowered, and certainly no competition for automobiles and busses. Then in 1949, the Budd Company offered a diesel-powered passenger coach with an attractive streamlined design, comfortable seating, and a high performance engine. The B-30 was the first Budd Car purchased by the NP. It was assigned to Spokane-Lewiston trains 311-314. Its performance record resulted in additional cars being purchased for the Duluth-Staples and Fargo-Winnipeg runs. Eventually, however, the loss of mail contracts and minimal public interest in riding by rail led to the abandonment of branch-line service and sale of the Budd cars to AMTRAK.

On a sunny Sunday morning, my brother-in-law "Sully" Sullivan with his two children Brad and Robin (on the left) and my two sons Tim and Jim were eagerly waiting to board the Budd car for a trip to Moscow, Idaho, while I followed along by auto, taking pictures of Number 311 en route.

Since his early days as an NP passenger train rider, Tim has logged a rather staggering total of world travel miles. After high school, he lived and worked in Germany for fifteen months and toured all of Europe, including Russia. Then, after college, he became a nuclear submarine officer with tours of duty on the attack sub USS *Cavalla* out of Groton, Connecticut, and the Polaris missile sub USS *Patrick Henry* out of Guam. He next went to San Francisco for two years as a recruiter, after which he joined the Naval Reserve and was employed by Johnson and Higgins, a New York based insurance company that has nuclear power plants among its clients. Business trips for J&H have taken Tim to London, Paris, Madrid, Brussels, Amsterdam, Seoul, Singapore, Kuala Lumpur, and more. It's been a long journey since leaving Oakesdale.

Milwaukee Road E-50 at Tacoma, March 23, 1952.

The Chicago, Milwaukee, St. Paul and Pacific, better known as the Milwaukee Road, was the last of the three northern transcontinental rail lines to be constructed. An advertisement in the June 17, 1909, edition of the *Tacoma Ledger* proudly proclaimed:

> The first revenue car freight over the Chicago, Milwaukee & Puget Sound Railway [one of the earlier names of the Milwaukee], Number 200116, household goods for Wm. Forrester, Tacoma from Chicago, Ill., arrived and was placed for delivery June 25th, exactly 8 DAYS Chicago to Tacoma. Through freight will arrive daily from now on and time will equal that of any other line.

Even though it was a staunch competitor of my beloved Northern Pacific, I always held a secret, envious admiration for the Milwaukee, probably because it dared to be different. Its biggest claim to fame was 650 miles of electrified track—Harlowton, Montana, to Avery, Idaho, and Othello to Tacoma in Washington. Its passenger cars were painted a gaudy orange, in contrast to the drab Pullman green of most other roads. Even in the diesel era, the *Olympian* was powered by flamboyantly designed Fairbanks-Morse engines.

The Milwaukee is long gone, but a number of my close friends had roots in this once great road. My daughter-in-law's father, Tom Sullivan, was for many years a Milwaukee special agent and remembered a wealth of fascinating stories about maintaining law and order on the "Trail of the *Olympian*." General Road Foreman of Engines,

Wayne Ferrier, and Engineer Frank Kobe, both Milwaukee men, attended the NP Historical Association gatherings. Bill Brodsky was a Milwaukee man before becoming president of Montana Rail Link and I often see Milwaukee Engineer Gordon Russ at the Washington State History Museum in Tacoma. Dave Sprau had the unique distinction of having worked for all three roads—NP, GN, and Milwaukee—and became a leading expert on Milwaukee Road history. Though not railroaders, two other friends made major contributions to preserving the Milwaukee's memory. John Finney, an Associate Dean and Registrar for the University of Puget Sound, completed an incredibly detailed study of the Milwaukee's Metaline Falls line, originally the Idaho and Washington Northern and later operating as the short-line Pend O'Reille Valley Railroad. Department of Defense Contract Specialist Wes Freeman procured many Milwaukee items for his superb railroad collection and became particularly knowledgeable about operations in the Port Angeles area.

The E-50 holds a unique niche in railroad history. Under the original number 10200, it was the first locomotive delivered to the Milwaukee by General Motors on September 25, 1915, and it became the focus of a massive advertising campaign using the slogan King of the Rails. It also powered the first official electric train out of Three Forks, Montana, on November 30, 1915. It now is preserved in the railroad museum at Duluth. Details of electric operation on the Milwaukee can be found in two excellent books, *The Milwaukee Electrics* by Noel Holley, and *The Electric Way across the Mountains* by Richard Steinheimer.

NP 2675, Class A-4, at St. Paul, Minnesota, September 15, 1946.

Two superb steam locomotives, rated among the best ever built, wait patiently at the St. Paul Union Depot for the two sections of the *North Coast Limited* to arrive from Chicago on rails of the Chicago, Burlington and Quincy. After replacing the Burlington engines, NP's 2675 and (behind her in the photo) 2674 will begin their grueling, high-speed race across Minnesota, the North Dakota prairies and badlands, and eastern Montana's General Custer-Calamity Jane territory. They will finally be relieved at Livingston by another pair of NP's fine passenger engines to continue the journey over the Rockies toward Seattle. This 1,008-mile assignment was widely publicized as one of the longest in the world without changing locomotives.

Livingston, Montana, in the glory-days of the NP, was truly a railfan's "heaven-on-earth." With every train, both passenger and freight, changing engines and with the bustling activity at the giant repair shops, there was an endless parade of power to be photographed. The surrounding mountain and plains scenery is magnificent, and it is in Livingston that Warren R. McGee made his home. Anyone with even the slightest interest in railfan publications has seen the credit line "photo by W.R. McGee." His lifelong friend and fellow photographer, Ronald Nixon, did a fine job of describing Warren in a 1952 article in NP's *Tell Tale* magazine:

> Conductor Warren McGee of Livingston, son of Engineer Howard McGee, has put together one of the largest collections of Northern Pacific engine pictures since he started photographing engines and trains in 1936. The following year he began the tedious but interesting task of locating old-time NP photographs. His work has not been of selfish

nature. Hundreds of railroaders stop at Livingston each year to go through his collection of prints, which bring back memories of an era that cannot be experienced in this age of Diesels.

> McGee is a very enthusiastic photographer. We have seen him run a mile at top speed for one shot of a locomotive—and we have seen him assume the most precarious of positions for a better view of a locomotive. He drives his automobile over rough roads to get action shots. He has traveled over the system many times endeavoring to get views of NP locomotives. On his honeymoon, Warren didn't pass up a roundhouse or a railroad yard, while his bride, Bernice, waited complacently as he toured railroad property.

I can testify from personal experience that the hospitality and generosity of the McGees had no limits. Not only did they provide me (and countless others) "room and board," but Warren's Model A Ford was always available to chase trains up Bozeman Pass in one direction and along the Yellowstone River in the other.

Two of my most unforgettable experiences were arranged by Warren. He told the engineer of a westbound freight at Laurel, Montana, to let me ride the cab of Class Z-6 Challenger 5107 to Livingston. We covered the 58 miles from Reed Point to Livingston in 54 minutes making it in for Number 2. On another trip, Warren put me in the caboose of a westbound freight at Livingston with a mammoth Z-5 Yellowstone helper behind. I can still remember the surging power behind the little "crummy" and the fear of being crushed if there was a sudden stop.

NP 2675 was constructed by Baldwin in 1941, and sent to Brainerd for dismantling on September 16, 1957.

McCarver Street Station, Tacoma, 1940.

I find myself having a unique status. I'm a genuine, living antique—a relic of a glorious era of railroading that has vanished. I'm a telegraph operator and a train dispatcher who plied his trade using "train orders" to direct the movement of rail traffic. For over a hundred years, train traffic was controlled by timetables implemented by written instructions (train orders) dictated by the dispatchers to operators at wayside stations, who would deliver them to passing trains using a bamboo hoop or a forked stick and string device so the train would not have to stop. Basically, these instructions informed a train where to go onto a side track and allow an opposing train or a faster train coming from behind to go by.

The train order system for rail traffic control was implemented not long after Samuel F.B. Morse perfected his invention in 1844. However, when the telephone arrived on the scene, the telegraph was relegated to branch-line use and as a backup for telephone systems on the main lines. When I started working for the NP in 1943, the telegraph was still a major part of the communication system, especially for the transmission of messages from, and to, division headquarters. But technology was growing by leaps and bounds—teletype, microwave, satellites, and computers. By the early 1960s, no more dots and dashes were heard in our area. The last working telegraph I saw was in an old CB&Q station in Galesburg, Illinois, in 1973.

The other major change in train movement control has been the adoption of radio, though it has taken a half-century for the full impact to be felt. Radios were first installed in engines and cabooses in the mid 1940s and at stations in the early 1950s, but were considered unsafe and unreliable for transmitting anything as important as train orders. The first radio *Rule Book* (1946) did not mention the possibility of using radio for giving train orders. Radio finally got its foot in the door in the April 1, 1954, edition, which stated:

> Train orders may be transmitted by radio when authorized under the following conditions:

> (a) To a fixed point when normal means of communication has failed. (b) to a standing train or engine in an emergency when normal means of communication is not available. (Such emergency to consist of casualties or accidents, engine failure, wreck, obstruction to tracks, washouts, storms or unusual delay due to equipment failure that could not have been anticipated by dispatcher before train has passed last open telegraph office, which would result in serious delay to traffic.)

Today, the telegraph offices and operators are gone, replaced by sophisticated electronic systems. Busy, main line territory utilizes Centralized Traffic Control, with the dispatcher lining switches and signals for trains by remote control. Written instructions are still being used in non-CTC territory, but now are called "track warrants" and are dictated over radio by a dispatcher directly to conductors and engineers who copy them down as their trains roll along.

In the days of train orders, one of the busiest operator's jobs on the division was McCarver Street Station in Tacoma, located in Old Town. All of the many southbound trains leaving Tacoma picked up their orders at McCarver Street until 1962, when it was replaced by the new UP Jct. on Dock Street at the foot of 15th Street, where the operator controlled all of the switches in the Union Depot area, as well as delivering train orders. Now even UP Jct. is gone, with a dispatching office in Seattle and later, Fort Worth, Texas, taking over this work.

McCarver Street Station was closed and UP Jct. opened at 8:00 a.m. on April 5, 1962. Carson Hickey on third trick was the last operator at McCarver Street. The last day-shift operator at the old station and the first operator at UP Jct. was Allen G. "Bud" Emmons. (After retiring from the NP, Bud became president of a local chapter of the Morse Telegraph Club. He also installed working telegraph instruments in museum depots such as at Snoqualmie, Tenino, and the Lewis and Clark Railway Station at Battle Ground. He arranged telegraph demonstrations at a number of fairs and expositions, providing a valuable service by keeping alive the bygone days.)

Magicians of Morse—The Railroad Telegraphers.

"Practice! Practice! Practice!" That's what Ted Williams said was the secret to hitting a baseball, and the same advice is true for learning to telegraph. At first, it's frustrating trying to make heads or tails out of a bunch of clicks, but after countless hours of listening a student will start to get the hang of it, and from then on it's a matter of polishing and perfecting. In a way, it's like learning a foreign language—once it's mastered, you can do it automatically without having to think "dit dah, now that's an A."

As with sports, some telegraphers are "naturals" while others struggle. Gifted telegraphers send code smoothly and evenly, and adjust their sending speed according to the ability of the receiver. When receiving messages, they can copy several words or even lines and carry on a conversation at the same time. At the other end of the scale is the "lid," who sends jerkily and runs letters together, and who is constantly "breaking" when receiving. Operators with the Associated Press, Western Union, Postal Telegraph, and railroad relay were the cream of the crop in their profession. Each railroad district and division headquarters had a large telegraph office where messages and reports vital to operations were sent and received—for the NP's Tacoma Division, it was the "WR" relay office on the concourse level of Union Station (every telegraph office had a one or two letter call sign). Up to six operators a shift were needed to handle the hundreds of messages from the various departments sent throughout the division.

Jack and Miriam Flagg and Pearl Jacobson were three of the finest operators ever to work in "WR." Their sending of code was beautifully clear and precise. They could copy anything sent their way, from the sloppiest operator who sounded like he was using his foot on the key, to the fastest and best of the professionals.

Jack learned telegraphy in the traditional way. He liked trains and hung around the depot at Kelso where the operators took a liking to him. They gave him basic training in code, rules, and station work, and then suggested he go to "WR" in Tacoma for advanced study. He broke in there with, among others, Louis Wiecking. Finally, after months of

intensive practice, he was pronounced ready, and on May 30, 1936, was sent to take third trick at Arlington. From there he bounced around the north end, working at Sumas, Sedro Woolley, Bellingham, Woodinville, Ravensdale, Kanaskat, Eagle Gorge, Lester, Easton, and Cle Elum. Then he heard that an extra 3:30 p.m. job was being established in "WR" and applied for it. It was highly uncommon for anyone with such limited experience to work in high-pressure "WR," but Jack was given the chance with the admonition, "if you screw up, you are all done." It was a struggle, but Jack survived and remained in "WR" until the opportunity arose to return to his home area. He was able to "bid in" to Longview. Finally, on June 1, 1961, he was named agent at Kelso, the highest position in the station where his career had begun.

Miriam's railroad education was more formal. During World War II there was a critical shortage of railroad workers. The Spokane Telegraph School advertised for applicants, citing the good pay and benefits. Miriam responded and upon graduation chose to work for the Tacoma Division of the NP. Her first assignment was at Bucoda. While there, her picture appeared in the NP's *Tell Tale* magazine with a story, which read:

> Full Crew—Handling station duties at Bucoda is a full crew of girls . . . Miriam Watson, First Trick Telegrapher; Margaret Bartholomew, Second Trick Telegrapher; Nellie Lutz, Clerk; and Iris Renn, Agent. These girls [the first two were graduates of Spokane and Miss Renn received her diploma from the Jamestown School of Telegraphy] are doing important work in railroad transportation during this war time emergency—so necessary to the big job of "keep 'em rolling."

Miriam followed the extra-board pattern of working many different stations on the division with the unique highlight of being agent-telegrapher at Wilkeson for a few weeks. Her natural Morse ability brought her into "WR." It was there that she met Jack, not in person, but on the wire, as he was at Longview. This story could be headlined

"Morse Leads to Marriage" as Jack Flagg and Miriam Watson were married in 1960. They lived for many years in the Rocky Point part of Kelso, close to the railroad.

In 1943, Pearl Jacobson left school teaching in Saskatchewan in response to the Spokane Telegraph School's search for students. The need for operators was so desperate at this time that the NP paid 42 cents an hour to anyone who enrolled. After she graduated and also selected to work in the Tacoma Division, same as Miriam, she was assigned to "WR" after short extra-board duty because of her exceptional talent at telegraphy.

The Spokane Telegraph School had a lasting impact on other lives as well. Engineer Sammy Waterson's wife, Betty, was a graduate, as was my wife, Cereta. As a matter of fact, we first met at the McCarver Street Station.

Another notable telegrapher was Duane Douglas "Duke" Tone, born on October 7, 1922, in his parents' home at 46th and L in Tacoma. Duke was Ralph and Nora Tone's first child, and was followed by sister Doreen and brothers Eugene, Raymond, and Darryl, all of whom were born at the old Northern Pacific hospital. He attended Horace Mann grade school, Stewart and Gray junior high schools, and graduated from Lincoln High School in 1940. His nickname during his school years was "Dude," but after becoming a telegraph operator, it was transformed to "Duke" because of an operator's careless sending of the letter "D," making it sound like "K."

Duke's first money-making endeavor was delivering the *Tacoma Times* from 1934 to 1938, while waiting to become old enough to follow in the family tradition. His grandfather and great grandfather were both brakemen for the Northern Pacific Railway. His father was a clerk for the NP for fifty years; first at the old Half-Moon Yard Office. For twenty years, he served as chief clerk at the Head-of-the-Bay Yard Office in Tacoma, retiring in 1968.

Duke's turn came in 1939, when he was hired as a call boy at the Tacoma Union Station. In keeping with the lot falling to most newcom-

Jack Flagg, Miriam Watson Flagg, and Pearl Jacobson at a Morse Telegraph Club dinner, April 27, 1962.

ers, Duke drew the midnight to 8:00 a.m. "3rd Trick." The callers' desk was not far from the "WR" telegraph office, and it wasn't long until Duke became a student of veteran wire chief and superb telegrapher Elise Mielke. Miss Mielke was a stern but kindly task-mistress, and within a few months Duke was unraveling the mysteries of Morse code. The next logical step for Duke would have been joining Bud Emmons and Dave Steinhoff at Lakeview for station clerical training (operators had other duties aside from telegraphing). However, the approaching war was thinning the ranks of board operators, and the legendary, garrulous chief dispatcher, Frank Kergan, said to Duke, "We need you now!"

Jim Fredrickson on duty at NP Mountain dispatcher's desk.

Duke Tone dispatching at Tacoma, October 8, 1975.

Nobody, I mean NOBODY, argued with Mr. Kergan! So off went Duke to Kelso on July 7, 1941, to be second trick telegrapher for the next two weeks. This was an extremely heavy-duty job for a newcomer, especially for one with no station accounting training. But Duke was a survivor, and went on to bounce around the division, relieving regular telegraphers at most of the stations. Among them were Renton, Cle Elum, Lester, Woodinville, 15th St. Tower in Tacoma, South Tacoma, Yelm, Bucoda, Saint Clair, McCarver St., Nisqually, Centralia, and all points south. The Grays Harbor branch has special memories for Duke, as he was not only telegrapher at Gate and Elma, but worked for a few weeks as temporary operator at Satsop and Brady while troop trains were bringing soldiers from Fort Lewis to participate in "war games." There wasn't even a station at these two places. An extension wire was hooked into the telegraph line, and Duke copied orders sitting on the vestibule steps of a coach, with his Morse instrument at his side.

A few years later in 1944, Duke's railroad career was interrupted by World War II when he enlisted in the U.S. Navy. First came basic training at Farragut, Idaho, and then off to the South Pacific on a troop transport, the former Matson luxury liner SS *Lurline*. He served aboard a supply ship sailing from Australia to the Philippines, and experienced a tropical typhoon. Arriving in Costa Rica, the ship loaded bananas, then sailed through the Panama Canal to New Orleans, Savanna, and finally, decommissioning at Baltimore. For Duke, the old slogan "Join the Navy and see the world" was the truth.

After the war it was back to telegraphing, with time off for study at the College of Puget Sound and Pacific Lutheran College. Then, on October 15, 1950, he started a thirty-two year career as train dispatcher at the Tacoma Union Station, adding up to a total of forty-three years on the railroad before retiring.

Much of my life story already has been related. Suffice to say, it has remarkable similarities to Duke's. I was born in Tacoma in 1926, peddled newspapers (*Tribune* instead of the *Times*), became a call boy for the NP in 1943, and then telegraph operator and train dispatcher.

NP's Tacoma passenger station in 1884.

When the first train arrived at Tacoma from Kalama, Washington, December 16, 1873, the station was in the Blackwell Hotel on a waterfront wharf below the present Stadium High School. At that time, Tacoma was located in "Old Town." A shack at 8th and Pacific and a logging camp between 11th and 13th streets were the only buildings in "New Town."

In the months following the arrival of the first train, Tacoma grew rapidly and soon 9th and Commerce was the center of town. The shifting of the city necessitated a relocated depot, and hopes were high for a great station occupying the entire block between Commerce and Broadway, and 9th to 11th streets. Instead, in September 1883 foundations were laid for the station at 17th and Commerce.

Tacoma was bitterly disappointed in the unimpressive little building, and it was promptly labeled the "Villard Depot" after NP President Henry Villard, who reputedly favored Portland over Tacoma. This began a twenty-five year struggle for a station the city and railroad could both be proud of, and finally on February 1, 1909, plans were finished and work began on Union Station. It was formally opened on May 1, 1911. The *Tacoma Ledger* proclaimed it the "new wonder of the west" and the finest station west of the Mississippi River.

Martin, Washington, November 1943.

Back in pre-radio times when traffic control depended on telegraph operators at wayside stations, Martin, contrary to its humble appearance, was absolutely essential to the movement of NP trains across the Cascade Range. The operators, both at Martin near the east portal of the Stampede Pass tunnel and at Stampede close to the west portal, had responsibilities found at no other stations in the Tacoma Division. In fact, Skyline and Blossburg at the Mullan Tunnel in the Rocky Mountain Division were the only other similar stations on the entire system.

It was considered unsafe to allow more than one train at a time to enter the long, two-mile, pitch-black tunnel, so movements between Stampede and Martin were controlled by a "staff" system. Located in these two stations were electrically connected machines loaded with grooved, round metal pegs called staffs. For an operator at one of the stations to remove a staff, the operator at the opposite end of the tunnel was required to push a release button. Thus, if an approaching train was next through the tunnel, the operator removed a staff and used it to unlock the train order signal and put it in proceed position (the westbound blade on the station signal in the photo is at stop position.) Then, on an elevated platform known as the "pulpit" close to the double track switch, the staff which had been placed in a tube on a wire hoop was handed up to the engineer or fireman (the broom on the pulpit in this picture was used for cleaning snow from the switch points). After proceeding through the tunnel, the engineer would throw the hoop off at the opposite station. When the train cleared the tunnel, the staff was put in the machine. While a staff was out, both machines were locked and remained so until the staff was reinserted, making it impossible for a second train to receive "staff" authority to enter the tunnel.

The operators at Martin and Stampede also were responsible for the correct alignment of the double track switch. The NP had a double track line from Easton to Martin and from Stampede to Lester, but it was single track through the old Stampede Tunnel. The engineers of trains emerging from the tunnel could not see the position of the switch until they were virtually on top of it. Often there would be a closely approaching uphill train, and an improperly lined switch could result in a head-on collision (I've heard of some close calls, but as far as I know,

this never happened). Another unique duty for the Martin/Stampede operators was the cleaning and issuing of respirators to each crew member of a train entering the tunnel. These were rubber masks, which had a wet sponge, to be used in case a train stalled in the smoke-filled tunnel. There were financial rewards for the extra duties at these stations—$2.50 a month for tending the double track switch, and $17.50 for "properly handling, caring for and cleaning the respirators and rescue apparatus."

When I first lived and worked at Martin, the population was seven. Section man Amobilio Innocenti and his wife occupied the house just beyond the depot. Then came a duplex with quarters for the first-trick operator, C.A. McGurk, and the second-trick operator, which was my home. Next was a boxcar converted to living quarters for the third-trick operator, Barney Roland. Around the curve, behind the bluff, was a house occupied by section men Narcisso "Scotty" Giometti and Foreman Vito Ferri.

Martin was no place for those who love comfort, what with outdoor plumbing, no electricity, and austere living quarters. Martin was accessible in the summer over a rough, dirt road from the Snoqualmie Pass highway, but twelve to fifteen feet of snow in the winter meant isolation, except for getting out by train. One unique feature of Martin was smoke. The two-mile-long Stampede Tunnel had ventilating fans on the west end (because of prevailing westerly winds) that blew the smoke from the trains out of the east portal at Martin. Two miles of smoke from as many as three steam engines on a train produced an immense, atom-bomb like cloud over Martin and its beleaguered citizens. It was perpetual grit and grime, and even necessary to keep kerosene lamps lit in the depot during the day, as the sun often was blotted out. Life at Martin didn't always seem like much fun at the time, but it's an experience I really treasure.

In the summer of 1991, retired operator-dispatcher and former Martin resident Ernie Harrison and I revisited our old home. It was enough to make old men cry—buildings all gone, and tracks removed except one main line, and it was partially missing. Little did we know then that revival was just around the corner—the Burlington Northern revamped and reopened the Stampede Tunnel in 1996.

"R" Manifest arriving at Easton, April 15, 1944.

The train of tank cars pulled by an FT-type road diesel was the "R" Manifest, the "second" most important train on the road at the time. The "R" Manifest consisted of empty tank cars returning to Texas for reloading. The "most" important train was its westbound counterpart, the "G" Manifest, loaded with gasoline and oil for the war in the Pacific.

Instructions from the general superintendent of transportation were brief and to the point—special handling must be given "G" and "R" manifest trains, and road and terminal delays must be eliminated. The almost brand-new, first-on-the-NP diesel normally would change off at Easton for a Z-6 Challenger (spotted on the cinder-pit track at the left). But, because of the "R" Manifest's high priority, the diesel here will go on through.

Incidentally, the man shoveling cinders in the photo brings back a special memory. He previously was a tunnel guard at Martin for wartime security, and he often walked down to Easton, eight rough miles, in his spare time and came back on a train. He and I struck a deal—he gave me meat ration stamps in return for my shoe stamps.

NP's "North Coast Limited" at King Street Station, Seattle, Washington, December 19, 1969.

The full story of the *North Coast Limited* would fill a book, but I will attempt to give a brief summary. In its early history, Northern Pacific was a leader in progressive railroading and the first to provide sleeping and dining car service to the Pacific Northwest. At the end of the Nineteenth Century, with passenger business booming, NP decided to inaugurate a passenger train featuring luxury equipment and service. The first run of the *North Coast Limited* came on April 29, 1900, from St. Paul to Seattle, with a scheduled time of 62 hours and 30 minutes. Many of the innovations on the train were new for western service and included observation club cars, barber shop-valet service, baths, steam-heat, and electric lights. These were "firsts" for its territory. Ten train sets of eight cars each were purchased at a cost of $800,000 each. Today AMTRAK is paying over $2,000,000 for one superliner car.

The main pride of these beautiful trains was the observation car. Northern Pacific was not bashful in its advertising:

> The crowning feature of this train is the Observation Car. By common consent it outranks anything of the sort in the entire country. It is the notable car of a notable train. The first forty feet of the car contain a gentlemen's toilet room; two smoking and card rooms each with six wicker chairs; buffet; barber shop; bath room; and a ladies toilet room, all opening on a side corridor. Then follows a space containing a library of 140 volumes and the current magazines; a writing desk with *North Coast Limited* stationery free; two open seated sections; and lastly the ladies parlor and observation room . . . The rear platform is 6-1/2 x 9 feet in dimensions. It is surrounded by an ornamental brass railing and is partially enclosed by the extended sides of the car.

Praise from the traveling public and the press was equally glowing. Count Kurt von Fersen of Germany was a passenger on the first run. The count noted:

> America has many surprises for us, and especially this magnificent overland train of the Northern Pacific Railway. It is a veritable palace on wheels and excels anything I have seen on the Continent or in America.

The Music Trade Review of New York City commented:

> The Northern Pacific system is splendidly organized and reflects the greatest of credit upon the management of that corporation. We have traveled on the famous *Sunset Limited* over the Southern Pacific from New Orleans to Los Angeles and we are impelled to say that the service there does not approach that rendered by its Northern Rival, where the traveler receives a full equivalent for his money, in service and in courtesy—a glaring contrast with our Eastern railroad systems of New York and New England.

Originally the *North Coast Limited* was intended to be summer-only service, but its instant popularity resulted in year-round operations, commencing in 1902. At first it ran only on NP rails, between St. Paul and Seattle, but on December 17, 1911, service was extended to Chicago over the Chicago and Northwestern. In 1918 the Twin Cities to Chicago leg was switched over to the Chicago, Burlington and Quincy.

Over the years, there was a continual upgrading of equipment and the adoption of faster schedules. Notable highlights include:

- Even finer observation cars were added in 1926—*Popular Science* magazine called them "A Luxurious Hotel on Wheels."
- New sleeping and dining cars came in 1930, and the train, for a short time, had Pullman sleepers only.
- The first, new, post-war lightweight streamlined cars were added in 1947.
- Radical changes came in 1952: the almost new lightweight cars were totally redesigned by the noted industrial designer, Raymond Loewy; and twelve hours were slashed from the schedule.
- In 1954 the first Vista Dome cars on a Northwest train were added.
- In 1955 stewardess-nurses joined train personnel, another exclusive service.

When AMTRAK selected its new routes, the most northerly (former Great Northern) line won out, partly because of the area's limited bus transportation service. Consequently the GN train name *Empire Builder* was retained by AMTRAK. The *North Coast Limited* had one final claim to fame. When it made its last run in May 1971, it was the oldest transcontinental "name" train in continuous service west of the Mississippi.

NP Class S-4 locomotive on connection to East Auburn for the "North Coast Limited," at Tacoma Union Station, January 15, 1954.

When the Tacoma Union Station was built in 1911, the passenger train was the only way to conveniently travel from one city to another. The planners for this magnificent terminal had no inkling of how soon the automobile and later the airplane would capture most of the passenger business. Northern Pacific owned the station, but it also was utilized by Great Northern and Union Pacific trains.

While researching old NP records at the Minnesota Historical Society, I was delighted to find a Tacoma Union Station timetable, dated May 20, 1914. It had been preserved by a stroke of luck. The president of the UP had written to the NP's president, complaining because the name Northern Pacific appeared above Tacoma Union Station at the top of the timetable, which allegedly violated the impartiality clauses of the contract. The offending timetable was included in the file.

Fifty trains a day were scheduled through Tacoma when this timetable was issued. Most had names that implied passengers would arrive at their destinations in a hurry. NP had the *North Coast Limited* and *Chicago Express* to Chicago and the *Mississippi Valley Limited* to Kansas City. GN offered the *Oriental Limited* to Chicago and the morning *Shore Line Express* and evening *International Limited* to Vancouver, BC. UP ran the *Shasta Limited* to California and *Oregon-Washington Express* to "All Union Pacific Points." Each road operated three trains a day to Portland. Aberdeen and Hoquiam were served by three NP and two UP trains. Numerous "locals," too, stopped at smaller communities. One could go by train to Wilkeson and Carbonado, Roy and Yelm, Kanaskat and Kangley. The common name for an overnight train in those days was *"Owl."* GN ran the Vancouver BC *Owl* and the Portland *Owl,* while UP had the O&W *Owl* and the Grays Harbor *Owl*. NP chose to be different, identifying its train as the *Portland Night Express* for its 1:40 a.m. departure.

New NP Vista Dome coach 550 on display at Tacoma Union Station, July 30, 1954.

In the mid 1950s, NP passenger service was well into the "Loewy" era, an exciting time considering what had happened immediately after World War II. For years Northwest travelers had been clamoring for improved "streamliner" passenger service. Finally, Northern Pacific, Great Northern, and Milwaukee said they would oblige, as soon as the war was over. However, when all three roads ordered new, lightweight equipment, there came a shock. The NP took the position that three fast trains between Seattle and Chicago would be too many. NP would keep the *North Coast Limited* on the same slow schedule to "conveniently serve intermediate communities," and the train would be a mix of the new streamliner type cars and the old heavyweights. What a disappointment!

This period of NP passenger train doldrums went on for five years and then suddenly there came a dramatic turnabout. In 1952 newly appointed President Robert S. MacFarlane announced "with satisfaction and pride" that twelve hours would be cut from the *North Coast Limited*'s schedule between Seattle and Chicago. Furthermore, the relatively new cars would be completely refurbished by world famous industrial designer Raymond Loewy; the old cars were to be removed and a fleet of Vista Dome cars would be added. Dome cars had been introduced by the Chicago, Burlington and Quincy on its streamliners and featured a glass-enclosed seating area above the roof level.

After being dead last in Northwest passenger train quality, NP could now boast in its advertising:

> There is only one train . . . yes only one train between Chicago and the North Pacific Coast which offers 4 Vista-Domes . . . such wonderful extras as the friendly attention of a Stewardess Nurse . . . the fascinating new "Traveler's Rest" buffet lounge car and diners serving famous meals including the "great big baked potato." Guessed the train? Right! It's Northern Pacific's *North Coast Limited*. One of the world's EXTRA FINE trains.

The first dome coach (the 550) from the Budd Company was immediately sent on an exhibition tour of key NP towns to promote the new service. After a day on display at Ellensburg, the 550 was next scheduled to go to Tacoma on afternoon train Number 5. This move happened to coincide with my day off, so, accompanied by my two sons and a friend,

John M. Coffee, I was aboard for the first dome car ride over the Cascades. It was a tremendous thrill!

Today the *North Coast Limited* is only a memory. After AMTRAK took over passenger train operations for the entire country, it chose to dispense with dome cars in the West in favor of superliner cars, which are inferior for sightseeing. A few Vista Dome cars still remained in service on eastern runs, but AMTRAK sold most of the fleet it inherited.

Mike Gelhaus, a BN locomotive engineer in Spokane, has had a lifelong interest in passenger trains in general, and the *North Coast Limited* in particular. He accumulated a wealth of historical data together with a fabulous collection of dining car china and other passenger car artifacts. In 1993 Mike took the ultimate plunge. He purchased former NP dome coach 549 and dome sleeper 313 from AMTRAK, with plans to restore them to their original elegance. This was a monumental undertaking, but Mike is one of those fortunate souls who has "true grit." The 549 was in relatively good condition with the NP murals still intact, as the doors were welded shut while it was in storage. The 313 was a sadder, but not hopeless case, having been stored in an unguarded location with the doors unlocked. It had been quite thoroughly vandalized.

The first problem for Mike was to move the cars from an AMTRAK shop in Beech Grove, Indiana, to their new home in Spokane. AMTRAK did not permit movement of retired cars on its passenger trains —they must go on freight trains. In November 1993, Mike asked me to accompany him on the journey from Indiana to Spokane because of my previous experience as a "rider." We trundled along slowly at first on a succession of Indiana short lines, but finally reached the Burlington Northern at Bushnell, Illinois. From then on it was smooth (but chilly) sailing. The cars were without heat, but we survived nicely with warm sleeping bags and four layers of clothing. Our timing was lucky. Through Minnesota, North Dakota, and Montana, the temperature hovered around 20 above, but a week later plunged below zero. When our train reached Savanna, Illinois, the 549 and 313 were back home on the same rail they once proudly rode on the *North Coast Limited*.

All during the journey, I had a deep feeling of irony. I had ridden on the first trip of an NP Vista Dome car in 1954, and here I was, four decades later, on board for the resurrection.

NP train Number 6, "Spokane Express" with Class A Engine 2608, departing from Seattle on September 15, 1945.

There are no trains left like Number 6, at least not in the United States. A real workhorse, first behind the engine are five passenger boxcars with LCL freight for Yakima, Pasco, Walla Walla, Spokane, and Pullman/ Lewiston. LCL (less than carload shipment) is no longer part of the railroad scene, with this business now having gone to trucks and fast freight companies. But in the days before United Parcel, the NP did endeavor to provide fast overnight service for small shipments.

Next in the train would be a half dozen or so baggage cars carrying mail and express. Then came a few coaches, a cafe car, and the Walla Walla sleeper, which was cut off at Pasco for further movement on Number 347. There was nothing glamorous about Number 6, though the ancient cafe car (half coach, half diner) had its own classic beauty with its mahogany woodwork and old-style plush seats. The meals were strictly in accordance with NP's dining car slogan, "Famously Good Food."

I loved the train. Many's the time I boarded it at East Auburn on my way to work the midnight shift at one of the isolated telegraph stations on the "Mountain"—Eagle Gorge, Lester, Stampede, or Martin. In my opinion, the most scenic stretch on the entire NP system was along the Green River from Kanaskat to Lester (before the Eagle Gorge Dam line change). The tracks crossed the river a number of times with superb views of rapids interspersed with emerald green pools. The highlight was crossing a bridge going into tunnel 8, then out onto another bridge, and into tunnel 7, and out again onto still another bridge. All of this could best be seen from Number 6 on a long summer evening, when the setting sun added warmth and golden light to the scene.

Number 6 itself was a spectacular sight struggling over the mountain

Engineer Nick Jacobs at Seattle, September 15, 1945.

grades with fifteen or sixteen cars. There would be a helper engine on the head end from East Auburn to Lester. At Lester, the Auburn helper was cut off and two other helpers were added for the climb to the top of the hill. Three mighty steam engines with their stacks blasting would have made a fantastic photo, but unfortunately, at this point, darkness had set in. With dwindling passengers, together with LCL and express going to the highways, Number 6 was discontinued in 1949 leaving behind only magnificent memories.

And now the rest of the story . . . The 2608 was a giant, but could go nowhere without a human hand on the throttle. Before Number 6 pulled out of Seattle, I took a picture of its engineer, Nick Jacobs. Engineers are commonly known as "hogheads" in railroad talk, but Nick was one of the elite group known as "throttle artists," who were exceptionally smooth and fast in their train handling.

One of my most memorable rides in a locomotive cab was with Nick and a Class A engine on the *North Coast Limited*. It's slow going over Stampede Pass with its curves and grades, but, once reaching the straight track at Easton, we went "like an arrow shot from a bow" in the words on an old railroad ballad. It wasn't long before the speedometer registered 80 mph. On the left was Highway 10 (ancestor of Interstate 90) and the automobiles looked as if they were standing still. On our right was the Milwaukee Road main line and just ahead was their premier passenger train, the *Olympian,* pulled by a Bi-Polar electric engine. The Bi-Polars were great engines for pulling trains over mountains, but were no match for a fast, high-drivered Northern. We easily won the race—an ultimate experience for a railfan.

NP 5117, Class Z-6, at Cle Elum, Washington, April 8, 1943.

In the days of fierce competition with the Milwaukee and Great Northern, Northern Pacific had two distinct disadvantages. First of all, by dipping down to Pasco, NP's route was almost one-hundred miles longer from Puget Sound to Spokane than its competitors' lines. Nothing other than building an expensive shortcut could solve this problem. A new line had been seriously considered years before, the Schrag Cut Off, but after laying only a few miles of track, the idea was abandoned. The other problem was a difficult one, but well within the realm of possibilities in solving—there was a critical need for larger and faster locomotives.

In the post World War I era, the steam engines originally assigned to freight service on the Tacoma Division for Stampede Pass were the Class Z-3 compound Mallets built between 1913 and 1923. They had the unglamorous nickname "sows," which tells a lot about their biggest drawback—a top speed of only 35 mph. Furthermore, they were wearing out. Competition demanded something much faster. As early as 1930, NP's mechanical minds were wrestling with a dilemma—a big engine that would fit through the ancient Stampede Tunnel. The mammoth new Yellowstone locomotives, largest in the world, were performing admirably in the Badlands between Mandan and Glendive and there were discussions about trying them out all the way to Auburn. After calculating the expense of strengthening track and bridges, as well as raising the height of water spouts and coal chutes for that distance, the idea was tabled. Then, in 1936 came the marvelous Challenger-type Z-6 5100s, slightly smaller but faster than the Yellowstones.

I have already described much of the Challenger story, but it warrants further telling. By 1939 the assignment of these beauties had been extended as far as Pasco, close enough to Stampede to warrant trial tests through the tunnel. The 5117 was selected, fitted with a special smoke-deflector hood for her stack, and during June, July, and August 1939 pulled trains through to Auburn. My good friend Dean Shannon was call boy at Auburn during the test runs and Albert Farrow photographed 5117 at Auburn with its unique smoke deflector.

The tests demonstrated that Z-6 operations to Auburn would require some track realignment and water spout raising. But there was one major obstacle—a Challenger had only a few inches clearance in the two-mile Stampede Tunnel, and, when working at full throttle, it produced an unbearable temperature of 130 degrees inside the cab. This resulted in one of the most fascinating of all test runs.

On August 10, 1939, 5117 with Conductor Harry Werner and Engineer Nels Eastman left Auburn Yard at 10:30 p.m. backing up, and ran "light engine" to Stampede just ahead of the hot-shot Merchandise train. When the Merchandise arrived at Stampede, its Z-3 road engine 4023 was cut off, and 5117 moving backwards pulled the train through the tunnel to Martin. With the cab leading, the temperature was a tolerable 88 degrees.

This led to what is probably the all-time leading "what might have been" for Northern Pacific motive power. Both NP and Baldwin Locomotive Works designers drew plans for a cab-forward locomotive similar to those used with great success by the Southern Pacific. But before an order could be placed, the cruelly efficient diesel locomotive burst upon the scene and the NP had what it needed—power and speed. It would be five years before the first diesels were delivered. In the meantime, Z-6 engines handled trains as far as Easton where they traded off with the smaller Z-3s, from Easton to Auburn.

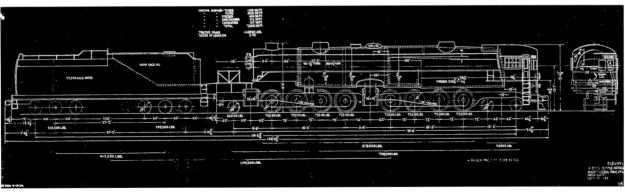

NP drawing for a cab-forward steam locomotive.

NP 2601 at Tacoma, July 4, 1954.

Locomotives 2601 and 2608 were marvelous machines, and were two of twelve engines ordered by the NP in 1926 to pull the *North Coast Limited*. They were the largest passenger locomotives ever built up to that time and proved to be an instant success.

NP naturally designated them Class "A" and proudly publicized them in this manner: "Riding the rails on 16 wheels, eight of them drivers, the new locomotive giants, measuring 104 feet in length, or as long as a third of an ordinary city block, represent an embodiment of the highest mechanical skill and the genius of modern locomotive designers and builders."

This description appeared on a postcard photo distributed by the NP. Other major railroads were quick to adopt the design, which was named Northern in honor of its origin. They performed with distinction for thirty years, but their fate was sealed by the coming of diesel. 2601 was the last to go—dismantled at South Tacoma on June 29, 1959.

Milwaukee Road Number 15, "Olympian-Hiawatha," pulled by Bi-Polar Electric E-4, Renton, 1949.

In 1923 the Milwaukee Road loudly boasted about the increased efficiency of its newly electrified territory where steam operations had been replaced. This set in motion a series of motive power improvement studies by the Northern Pacific lasting fifteen years. The NP was unimpressed by the Milwaukee's claims. It was felt that the steam vs. electric comparison differential was inflated because of the inferior quality of Milwaukee steam engines. Furthermore, the electrified territory between Harlowton and Deer Lodge, Montana, only had been in service seven years, and Tacoma to Othello just three years; thus the NP considered the statistics to be incomplete.

Shortly after receiving the mammoth new Yellowstone Class steam engines in 1930 for North Dakota and Montana, attention shifted to bigger and better steam engines for the NP's west end. General Manager W.C. Sloan to Vice President of Operations H.E. Stevens stated: "The cost of providing steam locomotives of sufficient capacity for use on our own line is prohibitive because of restricted clearances in tunnels and the limited capacity of bridges. So, as I see it, the only answer is electric operation between Auburn and Easton, if not Yakima."

Sloan also felt costs had significantly changed since their original look at the Milwaukee operation and it was time to do it again. For the next five years, the situation was analyzed and reanalyzed. Westinghouse Electric Company assigned a team of their experts to present a prospectus.

A number of fascinating concepts and considerations stand out in the correspondence files:

- An adequate electric power supply system naturally was a concern, but it was presumed that the new Grand Coulee and Bonneville dams would provide inexpensive and readily available electricity. However, a steam generated electric power plant at Roslyn using coal from NP owned mines was considered as an option.
- There was much talk about coordinating with the Milwaukee and having both roads use the existing electrified Milwaukee or abandoning that line and utilizing a newly electrified Northern Pacific route. The Milwaukee 3,000-volt DC system already was considered obsolete and NP electrification undoubtedly would be 11,000 volts AC. The Milwaukee had easier grades over the Cascades, but the Northern Pacific route was considered less prone to slides and washouts. However, any talk of abandoning NP track led to fears of Land Grant violations.
- The possible electrification of parallel lines prompted fears of criticism, especially from the U.S. government, which could regard it as an unnecessary duplication and waste of resources.

Finally, in late 1939, seven plans for revised NP operations were put on the table along with the relative operating costs:

- Plan A—Continue the present Z-3 Mallet steam engine operations.
- Plan B—Run via the Milwaukee between Renton and Easton with electric locomotives of either NP or Milwaukee ownership. Steam engines would handle trains between Auburn and Renton, and Easton and Yakima.
- Plan C—Operate over the Milwaukee between Renton and Easton, but use modern Class Z-6 steam engines between Auburn and Yakima, with an electric helper from Renton to Hyak at the summit of Snoqualmie Pass.
- Plan D—Complete electrification of the Northern Pacific from Auburn to Yakima, based on the Westinghouse study.
- Plan E —Electrification from Auburn to Easton and with steam power beyond.
- Plan F—Electrification only of the helper district, Easton to Lester.
- Plan G—Steam operation between Auburn and Yakima with both road and helper engines of the Yellowstone design modified for passing through the Stampede Tunnel (i.e., cab forward).

Also briefly mentioned in all of the studies was a new, low-level tunnel to be shared by the NP and Milwaukee and possibly even by a highway. The idea was quickly dismissed because there were "too many other extensive construction commitments elsewhere."

However, before any of these proposals could be implemented, they were buried under the avalanche of yet a newer plan—Plan DE which stood for diesel operation. The rest is history.

"North Coast Limited" day-coach section approaching Martin and the east portal of the Stampede Pass tunnel.

To pass the time of day on March 15, 1945, while waiting for my operator's shift to begin at 4 p.m., I walked to the east end of Martin, climbed up on the water tank, and photographed the second section of the *North Coast Limited*. The first section with Pullman sleeping cars already had gone by. The second section normally only had coaches, but with World War II still raging in the Pacific, the fourth and fifth cars are troop sleepers, mass produced to haul servicemen.

The Class Q-6 steam road engine could only pull five cars up the grade by itself, thus new diesel helper engine 6001 was added to the nine car train at Easton. Second 1 is on the westward main track. There also was a westward siding, eastward main track, and eastward siding. A train record sheet I have for one day in 1942 shows 10 eastward and 11 westward trains, plus 18 "light" helper engines for a total of 39 movements at Martin.

An August 18, 1915, letter written by the mayor of Kelso, C.O. Talbert, to NP Tacoma Division superintendent, W.C. Albee, reminds me of my experiences at the Kelso Station. The mayor was appealing to the NP to make improvements in the Allen Street grade crossing (estimated cost, $75.00). A traffic count for this "most traveled street in the city" was included in the letter:

May 15, 1915—	
Wagons and teams	130
Automobiles	52
Foot passengers	1347
Cattle	8
Horseback	41

How times have changed. Tom Gorman of the Kelso city engineers office has given me modern-day daily traffic figures for the Allen Street crossing: automobiles—21,475! The other categories are no longer applicable. Furthermore, the old Allen Street bridge was scheduled for replacement at an estimated cost of $12,000,000.

Now, to jump back to May 29, 1945, which was my most miserable day as an employee of the Northern Pacific Railway. I had attended graduation exercises at Tacoma's Stadium High School on the previous evening. After the ceremonies, my friends began to celebrate. I went to Union Station to board the midnight Owl, Number 402, to go to Kelso and be first trick telegrapher as the regular operator wanted a day off. I had been put to work because I could fill the most basic requirement (i.e., copy train orders from a dispatcher over the telephone) and had been told to do the best I could in regard to learning Morse code on my own (World War II, of course, had created desperate manpower shortages for the railroad). Learning to communicate with clicks is not easy and I was still struggling with it.

Jamie and Julie Fredrickson.

Kelso was a busy station in those days. Trying to copy messages by Morse code from the NP, GN, and UP relay offices was bad enough, but working with the Western Union proved to be absolute misery. For the most part, railroad operators were somewhat patient, but Western Union operators were just plain mean (it seemed to me at the time) and had only one sending speed—fast. Much of my day at Kelso was spent on the phone taking messages that should have come over the wire. More than once that day I heard the words, "What's the matter kid, can't you telegraph?" along with other unprintable comments.

Fifty years later, on June 18, 1995, I had a much more pleasant visit to Kelso. My wife Cereta and I are faithful fans of our twin granddaughters, who are fast-pitch softball players. Jamie and Julie had been playing since they were eight years old and the progress they and their teammates had made was impressive. During the school year, they played for Bellarmine High School (Julie pitched and Jamie played second base). In the summer, they played for the Tacoma Stealers, which participate in tournaments as well as the Tacoma MetroPark League. During a break between games in a Longview tournament, we drove across the Allen Street bridge for a look at the station where I had worked so many years before. The railroad and AMTRAK no longer had people assigned at the station; in fact, it had been turned over to the city. With the help of federal and state funds, it was being restored to its original glory to become a transit center for AMTRAK, Greyhound, and city and tour buses. Retired NP/BN Kelso Agent Jack Flagg was providing invaluable assistance for the restoration. After inspecting the station, we returned to the ballpark to watch our team take first place after defeating a strong rival, 2 to 1. The thrill of victory sure was better than the agony of beginning telegraphy.

This SDP-40F locomotive was only a year old and the Kingdome was being built at the time this photograph was taken. Hopes were high for the success of both, but each proved to be a disappointment (the Kingdome was razed in 1999).

The 531 was one of 150 locomotives ordered to provide both speed and power for the varied terrain of AMTRAK's long distance passenger hauls. Before long, however, an aggravating problem developed; they seemed inclined to "jump the track." AMTRAK maintained it wasn't the fault of the locomotives, but the "freight lines" over which AMTRAK operated thought there must be something wrong with the tracking of the trucks (wheel sets). Some roads limited these engines to 40 mph on curves exceeding two degrees. A few freight roads banned them altogether. Several tests were conducted seeking out the problem, but nothing was proven conclusively. In the early 1980s, AMTRAK traded them in for F-40s, which since have made up a substantial part of the locomotive fleet.

Ironically, many of the traded-in engines were geared for freight service and were sold to a number of freight railroads. They continue to provide reliable power for the Burlington Northern and Sante Fe.

The Kingdome was the former site of the Class AAA state high school basketball tournament, which reminds me of one of my favorite sports legends of the Northern Pacific Railway. In the late 1930s, an intense but friendly rivalry developed between the Auburn High School boys' basketball team and two teams at Lester—the high school team and the town team. Most of the players on both sides came from railroad families or were employees of NP. A few of the Auburn boys weren't from railroad families and did not have passes to ride the passenger trains. To solve this problem, the entire team would "play hookey" on Friday, climb into a gondola car, and take a free ride to Lester. Tom Strand remembered on one occasion that the Auburn High School superintendent was standing at the Auburn-Black Diamond crossing, taking the names of the boys as the train passed by. There was a meeting of all involved in his office on the following Monday.

The intrepid gang from Auburn would square off against the Lester High School team on Friday night and the town team on Saturday night. This was in the days of a center jump after each basket. Two scores that Tom remembered were: Auburn 40, Lester High School 9; and Auburn 39, Lester town team 23. The games were the entertainment highlight of the year, and the entire town turned out for a dance after the Saturday night contest.

Most of the players on both sides had lifelong careers with NP and BN. From Auburn were Chuck Hough, Dean Shannon, and Tom and Don Strand. Don O'Brien, Larry Meade, and Bob Hayes were the "nonrails" on the team. Lester High School had future railroaders Clayton McLean, Matt Fioretti, Tony Manicke, Ray Terlicker, Bill and Bob Noble, Ernie Ufer, Bob and Ed Rooks, and Ed Nash from railroad families. Bob and Tom Bush were the sons of a local dairy farmer.

The Lester town team reads like a "Who's Who" of NP locomotive engineers: Harry Iverson, Dutch Manicke, Homer McElreath, Bill and Bud Saunders, Jack Schmidt, and Art Steele. Vent plant operators from Stampede, Ted and Walt Rooks, also participated.

Clayton McLean and Homer McElreath did double duty. They played in the Lester town orchestra for the dances following the games.

Burlington Northern Number 139 leaving Tacoma, June 4, 1970. The consist included SP&S 860, 869, 866, and NP 337 pulling 57 loads, 42 empties, 4,795 tons. This train ran from Seattle to Klamath Falls.

"Alien Invaders Capture NP Geep" is the headline I would use if this were a tabloid publication. The fact of the matter is the Spokane, Portland and Seattle locomotives were alien to Puget Sound, but were not invaders—just new partners. Three months prior to this photo, on March 3, 1970, the Northern Pacific; Great Northern; Chicago, Burlington and Quincy; Pacific Coast; and Spokane, Portland and Seattle joined together to become Burlington Northern. A short time later, the locomotives were assigned their BN numbers—4108, 4126, 4120, and 1922.

The Spokane, Portland and Seattle opened in 1908 as a joint venture of the NP and GN to give them direct access from Spokane and Pasco to Portland along the north bank of the Columbia River (it never was extended to Seattle). Over the years, its steam engines were castoffs from the parent NP and GN, though in the late 1930s and early 1940s it acquired a fleet of superb new 4-8-4 Northern and 4-6-6-4 Challenger type engines identical to NP's A-3s, Z-6s, and Z-8s.

After diesels took over, the SP&S fleet primarily was made by the American Locomotive Company, while NP and GN mostly used units from General Motors and General Electric. SP&S historian Walt Grande asked an SP&S vice president if there was a reason why his company favored ALCOs. The response: "The Presidents of the GN and NP thought they should purchase some ALCOs because of the Elkins [Anti-trust] Act, but they didn't want them on their own lines so they bought them for the SP&S."

Almost immediately after the merger, the locomotive rosters of the component roads were intermingled. In just a few days, CB&Q units as well as yellow SP&S engines were common sights on trains. Engineers and train dispatchers soon found out why the NP and GN had shied away from ALCOs—they were prone to failure. Also, they were easy to recognize from the clouds of black smoke they belched. Some may argue that the engineers were not familiar with the engines or that they simply were worn out. For whatever reason, their life span on the BN was not long. Some were scrapped and others sold or traded in for new General Electric and General Motors locomotives.

I had one more opportunity to photograph SP&S 860, the lead engine in the photo. You would never guess where. It was in Speonk, New York, seventy-three miles east of New York City, on June 14, 1988, pulling a passenger train on the Long Island Railroad. It looked really spiffy in LI's blue and white and sporting a new number—LI 616. Long Island had purchased six of the former SP&S ALCOs after they were rebuilt. Small world!

$$ INDEX $$